Walk!

Tenerife

D1721655

with

David & Ros Brawn

DISCOVERY WALKING GUIDES LTD

Walk! Tenerife
First Edition - September 2006
Reprinted - March 2008
Second Edition March 2012
Copyright © 2012

Published by
Discovery Walking Guides Ltd
10 Tennyson Close, Northampton NN5 7HJ,
England

Maps
Map sections are taken from **Tenerife Hikers'
Maps** published by Discovery Walking Guides Ltd

Photographs
All photographs in this book were taken by the
authors.

Front Cover Photographs

Euphorbia atropurpurea (Tenerife
endemic common in the south and
west)

The Big One (Walk 38)

Walk 31 Arenas Negras   In Tenerife's western mountains

ISBN 9781904946823

Text, maps and photographs © David & Ros
Brawn

Walk! Tenerife

CONTENTS

THE WALKS

WALKS IN THE NORTH

WALKS IN THE SOUTH

ANAGA MOUNTAIN WALKS

THE AUTHORS

David and Ros Brawn moved to southern Tenerife in the spring of 1988. Finding a large resort filled with 'lost' tourists their first project was to produce the first integrated street plan of Las Americas/Los Cristianos whose current editions continue to provide the resort mapping that everyone uses - see 'Geranium Walk'. Discovering the resort hinterland resulted in the first 'Warm Island Walking Guide' for Tenerife South closely followed by guides for the North and West, then La Gomera and so Discovery Walking Guides was born.

Over two decades later, David & Ros have hundreds of books and maps to their credit and despite having to split their time between the DWG office (UK) DWG research (mostly Spain and its islands) and Australia's Sunshine Coast Hinterland (Maleny) they still think of Tenerife as their 'Home' island.

Having pioneered the use of GPS for walkers they have surveyed and mapped many of DWG's destinations to produce the 'Tour & Trail' series of maps used to illustrate Walk! guide books and the popular 'Bus & Touring' maps. Along the way David became a member of the British Cartographic Society including contributions to its Maplines magazine.

Destinations covered by David & Ros for DWG include; Tenerife, La Gomera, Lanzarote, Gran Canaria, El Hierro, La Palma, Madeira, Mallorca, Menorca, Alpujarras, Sierra de Aracena, Axarquia and Costa Blanca Mountains.

Acknowledgements

Our thanks to everybody who uses our books and maps and who take the time to update us with the latest on the ground 'trail' information along with their suggestions and corrections, which are invaluable in keeping our walking routes and mapping accurate and up to date. For Walk! Tenerife there are extra thanks to Joe Cawley (walks 39 & 40) and Stewart Bradley (Walks 20, 23 updating & 24) plus John Thorn, who managed to walk the GR131 before we did.

TENERIFE - A WALKER'S ISLAND

Tenerife is a big island - 2034 square kilometres big. It offers the walker a wide variety of landscapes to choose from; everything from coastal strolls, high altitude summits, pine forests and laurel forests, challenging and strenuous routes to easy country walks.

Your choice of routes will probably be influenced by where you are based. Major roads are generally of a good standard, and public bus services are efficient, clean and reliable. Taxis are reasonable value. Even so, to travel for two or three hours to reach a walk (and back again) can be tedious, so it is best to choose your accommodation to suit your walking needs. Notes on access for each route by bus and/or car are included in each walk introduction.

THE NORTH

Teide, from Pista Monte Pino (Walk 3)

The original tourist area of Tenerife offers accommodation of all types around **Puerto de la Cruz** giving easy access to the **Orotava Valley** which climbs up from the north coast until it meets the northern reaches of the **Parque Nacional de Teide**. There are fine coastal walks in this area, most of which are clearly sign-posted and easy to follow (ask in the local Tourist Offices).

Our six varied routes concentrate on the higher altitude areas around **La Caldera**, **Aquamansa**, **La Florida** and **Santa Ursula** which offer plenty of walks through pine forests and along forest tracks and walking trails, with fine views in clear weather.

THE SOUTH

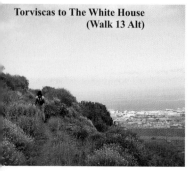

Torviscas to The White House (Walk 13 Alt)

There's plenty of accommodation in the sunny southern resorts of **Los Cristianos**, **Playa de las Américas**, **Costa Adeje** and **Playa Fañabe**, and plenty of variety for walkers. We offer fourteen diverse routes; coastal discoveries, forest walks, mountains and *barrancos*, villages and untouched wild countryside. Experience 'Wow! Spectacular to Adeje', 'Table Mountain',' Adeje Skywalker', 'Fantasia' and 'Taucho Tour' routes (and the rest).

We guarantee that southern Tenerife will never seem the same again.

THE WEST

Masca village, Walk 28

Our exciting selection of eight walks includes mountain routes and rugged country hikes in this unspoiled region of the island. The west can be reached by car or bus from the northern and southern resorts, and from the west coast resort areas of **Los Gigantes**, **Playa Santiago** and **Playa de la Arena**.

Drivers may have problems finding parking near **Masca** for our 'Survival Of The Fittest' route, and at the start of 'Picnic At Hanging Rock', so start out early.

CENTRAL TENERIFE

On Walk 37, 'The Big One'

If you want to stay in the centre, there's only one choice; the **Parador Nacional**. Otherwise you can reach **Las Cañadas** by public bus from **Puerto de la Cruz** on the north coast, or from **Playa de las Américas** in the south. Drivers will usually find parking near the walking routes. Our nine walks include some of the most exciting mountain and *cañadas* routes within the National Park and also two contrasting 'Lunar Landscape' routes, as well as 'The Big One - Crater Rim Challenge'.

THE ANAGA

Never mind that it takes a bit more effort to get to, the **Anaga** offers wild beauty, tiny hamlets, soaring peaks and plunging *barrancos*.

We guarantee that you'll never forget walking in the remote north-east of the island. Our six memorable routes take in **Taborno**, **Chamorga**, **Las Carboneras** and **Las Mercedes** and more. Visit the most remote hamlet on the island, see some of the rarest endemic plants and experience some of the best views and most extreme geology in the Canary Islands.

Looking back to Chamorga (Walk 43)

WALK LOCATOR MAPS

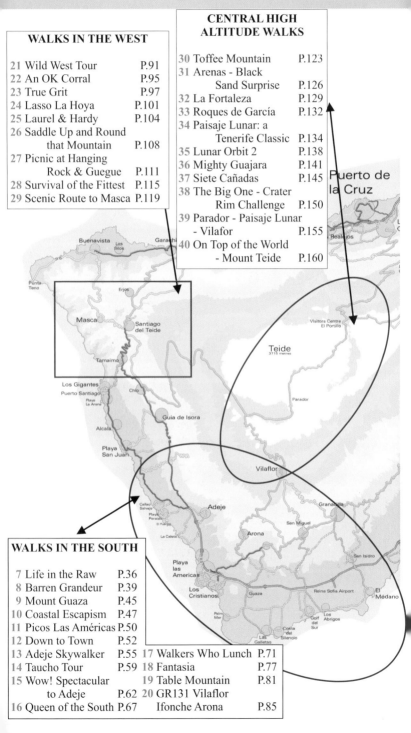

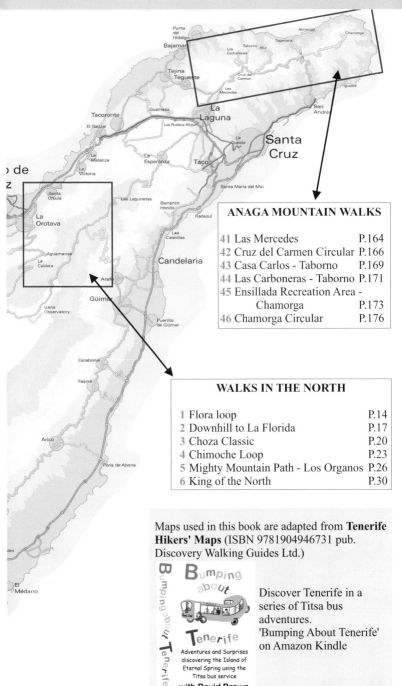

ANAGA MOUNTAIN WALKS

WALKS IN THE NORTH

Maps used in this book are adapted from **Tenerife Hikers' Maps** (ISBN 9781904946731 pub. Discovery Walking Guides Ltd.)

Bumping
about
Tenerife
Adventures and Surprises
discovering the Island of
Eternal Spring using the
Titsa bus service
with David Brawn

Discover Tenerife in a series of Titsa bus adventures.
'Bumping About Tenerife' on Amazon Kindle

The map sections used in this book are taken from **Tenerife Hikers' Maps** (ISBN 9781904946731) for all walking routes except 37 and 40. Map sections are aligned so that north is at the top of the page. Waypoint positions and numbers refer to the walking route shown in that map section.

Tenerife Hiker's Maps consists of large scale (1:25,000 and 1:30,000 scale) full colour maps. For more information on DWG publications, visit:
www.walking.demon.co.uk   www.dwgwalking.co.uk

Altitude

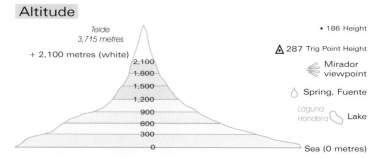

Roads, Tracks & Trails

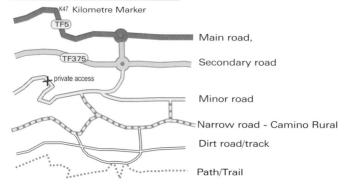

Walking Routes

GPS reception is generally good on all of our walking routes included in our new edition of Walk! Tenerife with the exception of Walk 28 in the **Barranco de Masca**. If it's your first visit to Tenerife then GPS will provide you with the pinpoint navigational accuracy you can rely on while discovering these exciting and adventurous landscapes, plus helping you quickly locate the start of each walking route. The GPS waypoint files for all routes (except 28) are available as free downloads from our websites at:-

http://www.walking.demon.co.uk/pnfs.htm
www.walking.demon.co.uk/pnfs.htm

Download the Walk! Tenerife zip file, then unzip the file into its 45 individual gpx files, then load the gpx file(s) into your GPS unit.

If you have a modern 'mapping' GPS unit such as an Adventurer or Lowrance Endura then you can use the digital edition of Tenerife Hikers' Maps to give you a real time mapping display showing exactly where you are on the walking route.

All of Walk! Tenerife's walking routes can be easily navigated without using GPS by following the detailed walk description for each route. However, using GPS gives you the added confidence of knowing exactly where you are on each route, especially if you are using a mapping GPS equipped with the Tenerife Hikers' Maps.

If you want to know about GPS and how it can help your own adventuring, or you are thinking of buying a GPS, then we recommend 'GPS The Easy Way' at £4.99 to give you a clear explanation of how these modern navigational aids work and can be used for your benefit.

 3 our rating for effort/exertion:- **1** very easy **2** easy **3** average **4** energetic **5** strenuous

 approximate **time** to complete a walk (compare your times against ours early in a walk) - does not include stopping time

 12½km approximate walking **distance** in kilometres

 250m / 850m approximate **ascents/descents** in metres (N=negligible)

 circular route

 linear route

 figure of eight route

 risk of **vertigo**

 refreshments (may be at start or end of a route only)

Walk descriptions include: timing in minutes, shown as (40M), compass directions, shown as (NW), heights in metres, shown as (1355m), GPS waypoints, shown as (Wp.3)

Notes on the text: Place names are shown in **bold text**, except where we refer to a written sign, when they are enclosed in single quotation marks. Local or unusual words are shown in *italics*, and are explained in the accompanying text or can be found in the glossary at the back of the book.

1 FLORA LOOP

The upper **Orotava Valley** is a popular region for walkers, where even on our introductory walking route we can surprise the old hands who stick to the traditional routes. These slopes are criss-crossed by walking trails and *pistas*, so it's very pleasing to find that Flora Loop covers paths not included in other walking guides.

'Introductory' does not, however, mean 'effortless', as in this steep landscape any circular route must involve a degree of climbing and descents. Very much a short 'forest and views' route giving us an introduction to the Orotava Valley.!

Access by car: easiest parking is at La Caldera car park then follow our route from Wp.9.
Access by bus: Nºs 345 and 348 to/from **Puerto de la Cruz** stop near the start point at the **Bar/Rest Aguamansa**.

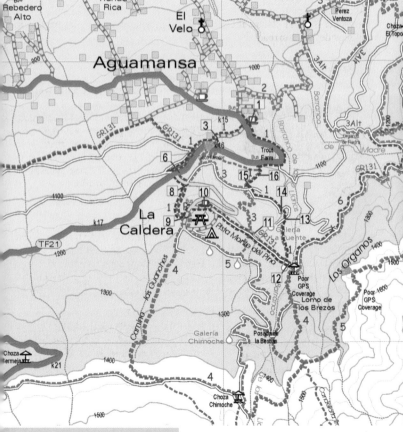

Our start point is at the **Bar/Rest Aguamansa** (0M) just above the bus stop, a good place for a coffee while drinking in the upper valley scenery; a contrast to the overbuilt lower valley. Across from the bar by the 'Las Fuentes 1000m' sign, a *camino rural* (Wp.1) climbs up from the TF-21 main road. We ascend it steadily, passing the green gates into the pine plantation (Wp.2 3M). The tarmac levels out at the gated entrance to **Granja Cinegetica Aguamansa**; a birds of prey breeding centre.

Opposite the wooden railings, a path (Wp.3 5M) is signed to **La Caldera**; taking this path, we're climbing through the green forest, passing above the chittering bird cages to a path junction (Wp.4, see Alternative Ascent) where we go right. We stroll along through the green wood with the TF-21 above us to come above a *pista* and a path dropping down to it (Wp.5 and an alternative route). Keeping straight on, we walk above the *pista* until we join it (Wp.6 12M) and turn left up to the main road (Wp.7).

Taking care crossing the road, we stroll past the picnic area at the start of the **La Caldera** lane for 110.5 metres (just shows how accurate our mapping software is!) to take a path up into the woods on our right (SSW Wp.8) signed 'Camino a la Caldera'.

Alternative Ascent
When at the path junction for waypoint 4, the path ahead holds the bleak prospect of the TF-21, but if you take this route you come out to a cleared area alongside the main road.

Disco Mirador

Take extreme care crossing the main road to go onto a path up into the woods. Take the red earth path to the right and climb up to a surprise; on a ledge overlooking the main road is the forgotten viewpoint of **Disco Mirador**.

Back in the sixties, before mass tourism, the well-heeled of **Orotava** would battle up the dirt roads to park in the cleared area and then ascend to picnic at the most outstanding view of the **Orotava Valley**; much more impressive than **Mirador Humbolt** lower down the valley. Concrete seats surround a grinding wheel table with breathtaking views when the valley is clear of cloud.

After this 'lost' *mirador*, not mentioned on maps or in guide books, we continue up the path, passing a minor path off to our left, to strike the *pista* that leads to **Galería La Puente**. Turn left and stroll along the *pista* to the **La Caldera** lane and rejoin our ascent.

Continuation

Camino a la Caldera may be signed, but due to water erosion it offers a rough ascent up through the forest. Keeping to a smoother trail to the right of the eroded official route, we climb up to an area of more mature pines where our path swings left, and the gradient moderates for us to come up to below a stone wall. Stone steps take us up to come onto the car parking area at **La Caldera** (Wp.9 24M).

After the stiff climb we go left to swing past the bar (Wp.10, refreshment stop allowed) to leave the tarmac as we head out on the broad **Pista Monte del Pino**. It is an easy stroll down this 'Orotava walking motorway' to pass a popular walking trail crossing the *pista* (Wp.11 30M) and a rough forest trail off to our right before coming to a walking trail dropping into the forest on our left (Wp.12 35M); just ahead is a *choza* and the **Chimoche** junction.

Going left, we pass a wooden spike discouraging vehicle traffic to follow the wide, boulder-strewn path down into woods. Away from the crowds on this little-used trail, we steadily descend through the trees, our route becoming clearer but narrower as we pass a 'sendero' marker and a tiny path off to our right before coming onto the *pista* serving the **Galería La Puente** (Wp.13 41M). If you go left you come to the *galería* tunnel and seating area in a few metres, making for a pleasant break in this floriferous valley. Across the *pista,* our path drops down to meet it again beside a white building and a *sendero* sign (Wp.14 43M).

Once on the *pista*, we cross the concreted watercourse for an easy stroll up from the valley, passing a smaller *pista* off to our right just before a major walking trail (coming down from Wp.11) crosses the dirt road (Wp.15 47M).

Turning right, we drop down the well-trodden path through the trees to face a simply enormous pine (Wp.16), just past which a trail goes left, a vandalised sign showing it as going to **Choza Dorta**. Our trail gets more water eroded before dropping us down onto the TF-21 by a *choza*-style bus stop opposite the trout farm (Wp.17 54M).

The enormous pine at Wp.16

A relaxed stroll alongside the main road, passing the **Camino de Candelaria** (Wp.18) on our right before arriving back at **Bar/Rest Aguamansa** (60M).

Starting with the N°345 bus to **Bar/Restaurant Aguamansa** (and the bus stop) this walk follows country lanes through lush vegetation and a couple of *barrancos*, down the eastern side of the **Orotava Valley**. The route is virtually all downhill, steep in parts but on tarmac lanes, descending from 1050 metres to 500 metres altitude through hamlets and villages. Although downhill is not energetic, it can leave an impression on the calf muscles and knees so treat this as a stroll and not a race. We make no excuses for this being an 'all tarmac' route as it passes through some exceptional pastoral scenery with exceptional flora.

Access by bus: The N°345 bus via the **Botanical Gardens** and **La Orotava** gives us a scenic ascent with spectacular views (sit on the right) across the **Orotava Valley**. Alighting at **Bar Aguamansa**, you might like to sample the atmosphere while taking refreshments on the bar's rustic terrace tables, from where you can soak up the views across the Trout Farm and pine forest and away to the mountains. Service at the bar is good except when coach tours arrive and chaos ensues for a few minutes.

Access by car: linear route so you can park near the start and use the 345 service to bus back to your car.

Our route starts at the bus stop (0M) and shelter from where we leave the main road behind as we walk steeply downhill on the small lane heading down to **El Velo**. We pass a tarmac lane on our right (Wp.1), then two hundred metres down the lane turn right onto the **Camino de Mamio** (Wp.2 3M), the second lane we come to.

Castanea sativa (sweet chestnut)

In a couple of minutes we're leaving the houses behind to come into open countryside, where the fields on each side of our narrow walled lane are dotted with bracken and chestnut trees (excellent nuts if you're here at the right time). This *camino* used to be a country track, but in recent years a tarmac lane has replaced the original donkey trail. Even so, the route retains its country charm despite the 'upgrading' for motorised traffic.

It's not long before we drop into the first of two floriferous *barrancos*. At the floor of **Barranco de los Llanos** the road forms part of the watercourse (Wp.3), which makes the route difficult (and not recommended) during heavy rain.

Climbing out of the first *barranco*, we stroll through the pastoral countryside, passing a lane on our right (Wp.4) before descending into the **Barranco de la Madre**, again with the road forming part of the watercourse (Wp.5 15M).

Leaving the *barrancos* behind, we come into a fertile area, lush with wild and cultivated plants. After passing a group of vegetable plots lined with fruit trees on our left, we bear left at a junction(Wp.6), keeping to the 'main road' as it passes between some small cottages and dry stone walls dotted with ferns. Down the country lane we come to the meeting of the **Mamio/Pinoleris/La Florida** lanes (Wp.7 27M, sign-posted and with a shrine on the corner). Our 'Walk 3, 'Choza Classic' route joins us from the **Perez Ventoza** lane as we keep left at the junction and continue gently downhill on the narrow lane.

We 're now getting well into the walk, passing a track on our right (Wp.8) and need to keep a sharp lookout for house N°68, **La Zaraza** (Wp.9), on our right - it's easy to walk past this house without noticing.

Immediately past the house is a junction (Wp.10) where we turn right onto the narrow lane of **Los Caminos**. If you miss this junction then continuing

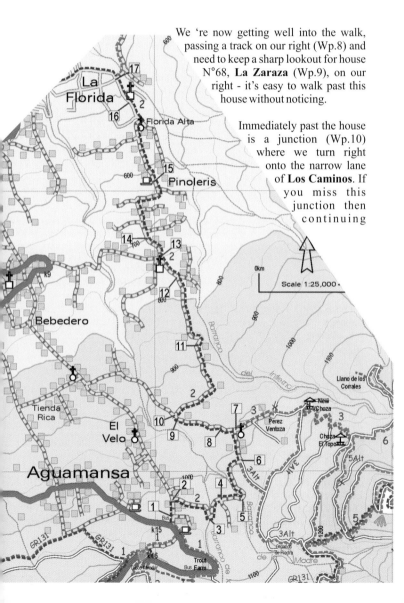

straight ahead on the main lane after **La Zaraza** would take us downhill to drop down through a steep and tight S-bend and into a *barranco*. Crossing the ravine on a little white bridge, we pass a shrine before coming into countryside similar to our main route but without the views. Continuing downhill the incorrect route is confirmed if you find yourself overlooking the main road at a hairpin bend by the **La Curva Bar** and K9 marker. If you do find yourself in this position, you can easily rejoin our 'correct' route by taking the street heading east (E) from the bar. Keep on the street and in just under a kilometre you will meet the correct route at a junction with a yellow sign for 'La Florida & Pinoleris'.

Back on the narrow lane just after **La Zaraza**, we stroll down through a quiet countryside of trees and stone walls. Densely growing foliage allows only occasional glimpses of the houses set back from the narrow lane, such as **Finca El Bosque** (Wp.11). As we continue downhill, the dense foliage gives way to vegetable plots and houses, allowing us extensive views over the eastern part of the **Orotava Valley** as we approach a T-junction marked by a bent 'Stop' sign (Wp.12 47M), where we turn left.

Sand coloured walls topped with geraniums line the right side of the road and we are soon passing a large picnic area and a church on our left as we come down to another road junction (Wp.13). The street from **La Curva Bar** joins us from the left as we keep right to follow the yellow 'La Florida & Pinoleris' sign. We are now passing through a grape area with vines covering the terraces, occasionally interspersed with vegetable plots. Far ahead, the small village of **Pino Alto** can be seen clinging high up on the edge of the cliffs which form the valley wall.

As well as enjoying the views, keep an eye open for an excellent example of a Canarian thatched hut with its eaves brushing the ground (Wp.14), while behind it dramatic pine forested mountain slopes rise steeply. Keeping to the main lane we come to another road junction where the **Bar Florida Alto** (Wp.15 62M) announces the high part of **La Florida**. Following the road round to the right, our route ahead drops steeply downhill in a straight line between tightly packed two storey houses decorated with flowering plants on the edges of their flat roofs. The end of the hill is marked by a church and school on our right (Wp.16), just before we come to the crossroads in **La Florida** (Wp.17 77M) with the narrow lane to **Pino Alto** dropping into the valley on our right.

This is a good place to enjoy the views and take a couple of minutes to decide what to do next, though the comfortable seat in the bus shelter faces away from the views, unfortunately. We've walked nearly five kilometres, and while the downhill route isn't very strenuous it can be hard on the legs. From where we stand the *camino rural* to **Pino Alto** drops to our right before climbing steeply (100 metres) into the village.

Our choice is to turn left and seek refreshment in the appropriately named **Bar La Tranquilidad**. Suitably refreshed, you could wait for the La Florida - La Orotava bus (hourly), but far better to walk off that food by strolling through this affluent village, dropping into and climbing out of yet another *barranco* (look for the pedestrian stairs), to meet the main road and wait for the regular and frequent bus service back to **Puerto de la Cruz**.

If one route characterises walking in the **Orotava Valley**, then it has to be the **Choza Perez Ventoso** 'Choza Classic'. Bus riders have the advantage over car drivers by starting at **La Caldera** but having the option to finish downhill to **La Florida** or **El Bebedero**; a far easier finish than the stiff climb up through **Aguamansa** to **La Caldera**. Easy route finding combines with good scenery and bucolic charm to create the valley's most popular walking route.

In wet weather the steep path down the valley wall from **Choza El Topo** becomes very slippery indeed. If you get caught in wet weather, not unusual in the **Orotava Valley**, then descend on the shortest alternative route by going down the *pista* signed to **Aguamansa** - see map.

Access by bus: Service N°345 drops you off at **La Caldera**.

Access by car: Park at the **La Caldera** car park, off the TF-21 between kilometres 16 and 17.

We start out from the **La Caldera** car park and bus stop (Wp.1 0M) to stroll past the bar and out onto the **Pista Monte del Pino** (Wp.2). Down past the trail of our return route, and of our Walk 1, 'Flora Loop' path (Wp.3), we pass the *choza* at the **Chimoche/Pedro Gil** path junction (10M) to continue along the broad *pista*. GPS users will find it best to walk on the left of the *pista* to reduce the effect of 'mountain shadowing' caused by the steep valley wall on our right.

Our route curves into and out of a small *barranco* before we come to impressively balanced giant rocks opposite a private chained-off track. **Pista Monte del Pino** now meanders along going gently downhill, with only occasional views through the trees, for us to pass a little-used path on our left before swinging down to round an impressive stone house (Wp.4 28M) sitting just above the **Barranco de la Madre**'s watercourse.

Over the *barranco*'s bridged watercourse, our route starts to climb steadily, water eroded in places, with the valley steepening on our left. Curving up to leave the valley behind, we come to the **Aguamansa** *pista* (Wp.5 35M) signed off to our left; if you opt for this alternative, then you're now at the highest point of your route.

We continue up the **Pista Monte del Pino**, steadily climbing until the *pista* reaches a crest, where after a flat section we're climbing again. It's a steady uphill, accompanied by impressive glimpses through the trees, all the way up to **Choza El Topo** (Wp.6 45M) with its *pista* and path cross-roads. At the *choza*, a broad *pista* climbs up to the right, an alternative **Los Organos** route, while **Pista Monte del Pino** continues ahead and a path drops down beside the *choza*. **Choza El Topo** is a popular 'motorway' rest point so you'll be lucky to find the seats unoccupied.

From **Choza El Topo** we take the path dropping steeply down the forested slopes. The path starts steep and gets steeper as we skitter down through a series of zigzags to a *pista* going left off a hairpin bend (Wp.7 51M).

The Aguamansa pista

By now you'll have realised why we don't recommend this route in wet weather, when you are likely to slither down out of control to arrive at the bottom looking like a pig in the proverbial.

More steep zigzags down past a *sendero* sign bring us down alongside a *choza* perched above the path on our right, just as we meet the **Aguamansa** *pista* (Wp.8 60M). This is the **New Choza** which most people imagine to be **Choza Perez Ventoso**; you should find space on its benches though unfortunately its table has been stolen!

From **New Choza** we continue downhill

... a beautiful view of Teide ...

on the wide *pista* to a beautiful view of **Montaña Teide** framed by the tall trees before dropping down to the **Perez Ventoso** marker (Wp.9). On the opposite side of the trail you can see the few remains of the base of **Choza Perez Ventoso** but the wooden structure finally rotted away in 1995, though it is still shown on some maps.

Now we come onto a narrow *camino rural* which takes us out into a bucolic landscape of farm plots and log cabins, enhanced by the flowers and white broom lining the narrow lane. Passing a concrete lane on our left (Wp.10) we stroll along to the shrine junction with our Walk 2, 'Down to La Florida' route (Wp.11 69M). Here bus riders can opt for an easy finish by going right, while we turn uphill for a steady climb up past houses to a junction where our 'wet weather' alternative (signed 'Organos de Piedra Aventura') comes down the concrete lane to join us.

Keeping to the tarmac lane (signed 'Aguamansa'), we stroll past a dirt lane to drop into **Barranco de la Madre**, and then it is up to pass a concrete lane on our left before dropping into the **Barranco de los Llanos**. Taking a walking trail (Wps. 12 & 13), we cut off a loop of the lane and then climb up the lane out of the *barranco*. Now it is easy strolling along the lane past the first houses to meet the **El Velo** street at the **Camino de Mamio** street sign (Wp.14 85M).

It's seriously uphill as we turn left to climb up the steep street to come onto the TF-21 by the bus stop (Wp.15 90M). Going left, we walk up to the **Bar/Rest**

Aguamansa and give in to the temptation for refreshments before tackling the climb up to **La Caldera**.

From the bar (0M), we cross the TF-21 to take the 'Flora Loop' *camino rural* up to the 'La Caldera' signed path (Wp.16). Climbing up through the woods, we keep straight on at the path junction (Wp.17) to climb up to the TF-21 (6M).

Carefully crossing the road, we take the path into the woods. Keeping right on the red earth path we climb up through the woods to a surprise; the little-known **Disco Mirador** (Wp.18) complete with seats and 'grinding wheel' table, not to mention an awesome view of the **Orotava Valley** when it isn't cloudy. Back on our path, we climb up through the trees, passing a smoother path off to our left (Wp.19) before emerging onto the **Galería La Puente** *pista* (Wp.20).

Once on the *pista*, the shortest route is to go right to the **La Caldera** access road and then take the 'Flora Loop' path for a stiff climb up through the trees to the **La Caldera** car park. We opt to go left for a gentle stroll down to where a major walking trail crosses the *pista* (Wp.21). Here we turn right to follow the broad path up through the woods in lazy zigzags, passing *sendero* signs before emerging onto the **Pista Monte del Pino** (Wp.22 31M). Going right, it's a gentle uphill stroll, retracing our outward route back past the bar to the car park.

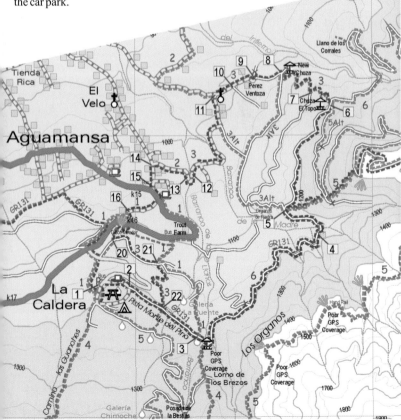

4 CHIMOCHE LOOP

An easy tour of the upper **Orotava Valley** taking in sections of classic walking trails before descending back to **La Caldera** by a little-known walking trail. Take your time on the strenuous climb up through the forest on the **Candelaria Trail** and you'll be rewarded with easy strolling to **Choza Chimoche** plus a relaxed descent back to your start point. Should you be caught out by bad weather, or find the climb too much, there are three options to shorten this route.

3 | 2H | 6 km | 240m / 240m | ↻ | 2*

* at **La Caldera**

Access by bus: Service N°345 drops you off at **La Caldera**.

Access by car: Park at the **La Caldera** car park, off the TF-21 between kilometres 16 and 17.

We start out from the parking area at **La Caldera** (Wp.1 0M) to stroll past the bar and round to the junction with the main *pista forestal* (Wp.2) signed 'Los

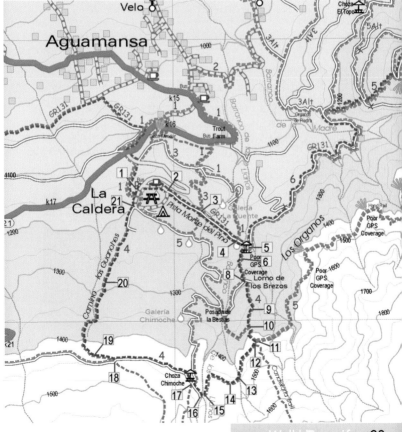

Organos'. It's an easy stroll down the broad *pista* passing a water pipeline and a walking trail crossing our route (Wp.3). Over a bridge, we pass a track off to our right (Wp.4) to come to a *pista* off to the left just before the *choza* and *fuente* at the 'Pedro Gil, Chimoche' signed junction (Wp.5 10M). Here we leave the *pista* to follow the clear signed path up into the forest.

Now it is across a watercourse and then we are into a relentless ascent through the pines and tree heather, gentle at first as we come up to pass the three crosses (Wp.6 12M) but then getting steeper as we zigzag up the valley wall. You'll need a top-notch GPS unit to keep satellite signals amongst all these trees and the steep valley wall, not that there's any danger of getting lost as there is just one clear path and we are on it.

Taking breaks whenever we need them, we gradually ascend up through the twists and turns to come to a clearer area by some large eucalyptus trees and a shrine set in the crook of a hairpin bend (Wp.7). Just a little more climbing brings us up onto a *pista forestal* at **Lomo de los Brezos** (Wp.8 25M) for a welcome break. You can shortcut the route at this point by going right on the *pista* and at a T-junction go right again to head down to **La Caldera**.

Across the *pista* from the **Lomo de los Brezos** sign, we go up onto a small walking trail which winds up amongst the trees in a series of zigzags. The trees are less dense than lower down, allowing good GPS reception. As usual, it is onwards and upwards on the relentless ascent, taking breaks whenever you need them, the magnificent **Los Organos** cliffs glimpsed through the trees on our left providing some light relief. There is so little to comment on in this bland section of forest that even a small rock outcrop (Wp.9) seems like a major feature, before we come up to a junction (Wp.10 40M). Here a broad earth path sweeps gently down into the valley on our right, our second opportunity to short cut.

Spurning temptation, we continue uphill through the thinning pines to climb into a region of black *picon* where our path goes up through a narrow trench before coming to a T-junction (Wp.11 45M). Here the **Los Organos** path comes in from the left; definitely not a short cut!

Aeonium holochrysum

We go right to continue up to come below a huge Canarian pine with a large red arrow sprayed on its trunk (Wp.12 47M). Don't worry - the upward route signed by the arrow is the **Candelaria** pilgrimage route, while we are now at the top of our relentless ascent. We pass the pilgrimage path on our left to stroll along above a tree-filled ravine. Our path undulates along to cross a picturesque rocky watercourse (Wp.13 50M) before climbing quite steeply to come above a sheer ravine, *Aeonium holochrysum* and other 'rock roses' of the Crassula family lining the small cliff on our left.

We head across the ravine's watercourse below a floriferous cliff (Wp.14).

Now our route starts to run gently downhill as it swings south alongside a sheer ravine, unusual as this is sheer earth rather than rock. Crossing the watercourse (Wp.15 56M), we round a ridge into a gentler valley to cross a pair of watercourses to come onto the end of a dirt *pista forestal* (Wp.16). Following this *pista*, we come along to **Choza Chimoche** at a junction of *pistas forestales* set in a forest clearing (Wp.17 59M), often busy so you might be lucky to get a seat, From the *choza* you can go north (N) on the right hand *pista*, the favoured route of most walking writers, to descend the broad dirt road past **Galería Chimoche** to **La Caldera**; our third and last opportunity to shortcut.

From **Choza Chimoche** we head west (W) along the track which gently climbs to give occasional views over the trees to the ocean. Ten minutes from **Choza Chimoche** a walking trail crosses the *pista* (Wp.18 68M) just before a large sign, 'Limite Aprovechamiento Vecinal'. We take the right hand path; although this junction is marked by small signs high up on the pine trees - 'La Caldera' right and 'M. Limon' left - it is easily missed, and the next junction is at the TF-21 main road!

Stepping off the *pista*, we come down into the green wood on a cobbled donkey trail, unfortunately littered with stones making for slow progress, then crossing a watercourse (Wp.19). Although technically part of the same forest this is a softer, greener woodland compared to the harsh pines and tree heather on the ascent up the **Pedro Gil** path. Our trail twists down through the trees in a steady descent, the trees closing over our route to form a green tunnel (77M); despite the tree cover we still have good GPS coverage.

After the green tunnel the woodland opens up as we cross a small watercourse, and the path is less rock littered. Continuously descending, the path stone-littered again, we come down to cross a water pipeline (Wp.20 92M), the woodland less dense around our route for a short section. Laurel trees supplement the Canarian pines and tree heathers as we continue down alongside moss-covered rocks to come to the end of the *sendero*, signed on a large pine, at a dirt *pista* (102M).

Going left, we come down the rocky *pista* to the **Caldera** road (Wp.21), the *pista* signed 'Camino de los Guanches', to cross straight over onto a woodland path which takes us through the wood, passing a path off to our right (Wp.22) before coming down onto the tarmac again at the parking area (105M continuous walking).

5 MIGHTY MOUNTAIN PATH - LOS ORGANOS

Northern Tenerife has one true classic walk, and this is it. Following an amazing woodland and ravine trail, we traverse the south-east wall of the **Orotava Valley**, taking in a surfeit of scenery, views, flora and orogenical geology. You need good weather and an adequate fitness level, but if you have these, then this is one route not to miss.

Some walkers are discouraged from this route by the 'alarmingly vertiginous' description given in some guide books, but as vertigo sufferers ourselves, we found no problems. There is a very short exposed stretch but even here a well fixed steel-pipe handrail gives confidence. Those 'other guide books' give rather curt descriptions for this route, while some of the few items they mention (guard rails at a viewpoint, Wp.21) disappeared years ago, so we take their 'vertiginous' warnings as being equally up to date.

5 · 4½ H · 13 km · 650m / 650m · ⚠ · ↻ · 2*

* at La **Caldera**

Access by bus: Service N°345 drops you off at **La Caldera**.

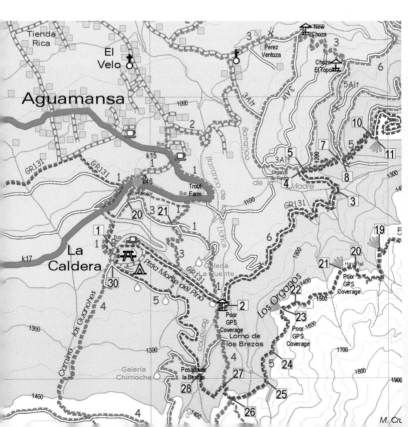

Access by car: Park at the **La Caldera** car park, off the TF-21 between kilometres 16 and 17.

We start from the **La Caldera** car park (Wp.1 0M) following the road past the

bar and out onto the **Pista Monte del Pino**, passing the *choza* at the **Chimoche** path junction (Wp.2 8M); by now you probably know this stretch of walking 'motorway' as well as your own footwear! We pass the balanced rocks and private *pista* before dropping down past the stone house to cross the stone bridge (Wp.3 27M), then labouring up the steady ascent to the 'Aguamansa' signed *pista*

Amongst mature pines

(Wp.4 30M); which seemed quicker than usual today.

Now the path finding and the exertions begin. Ten metres past the *pista*, a faint and easily missed dirt path climbs up into the forest (Wp.5). The path is poorly defined in places, a couple of small cairns providing guidance in deciding which is path and which is water runoff, as we climb steeply up through the pines and tree heather in a 'puff and grunt' ascent to a large pine whose roots

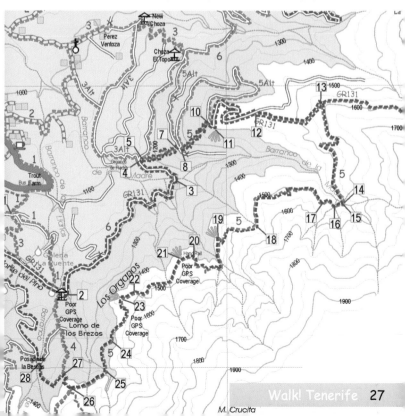

make steps in the path (Wp.6). From the large pine we climb up steeply through hairpin bends before emerging onto the broad *pista* coming up from **Choza El Topo** (Wp.7 47M). If walking the route in reverse, we recommend using the *pista* rather than the steep woodland paths.

Going right, we step onto another faint path (Wp.8) which climbs up from the *pista* junction. Again, it is steeply up through the pines and heather, another 'puff and grunt' ascent which brings us up to a small clearing (Wp.9 57M) amongst mature pines with comfortable rocks. From the clearing our path seems to get even steeper as we labour up to climb onto the *pista* again (Wp.10 68M). After the steep ascents, the *pista* makes for a relaxed stroll which brings us in a couple of minutes to a 'seat height' rock with panoramic views of **Teide** (Wp.11 70M). An easy stroll takes up the track to its crest and there's even a gentle downhill before coming to the rock arrow (Wp.12 82M) pointing us off the *pista* onto the **Organos** path.

We're amongst mature pines, soon climbing steeply again before coming onto a broad *lomo*, after which we are back to a 'puff and grunt' steep climb going up through zigzags to a long climbing traverse which brings us out of the trees to a 'rock gate' (Wp.13 100M). Just above the 'rock gate' we reach a junction with green arrow waymarking.

Going right, we are immediately rewarded with a pleasant woodland path which contours along with magnificent views before starting to descend below a cliff (poor GPS reception) to a hairpin bend. Our path drops down through another hairpin (Wp.36) before our steep descent runs out for us to cross a water runoff (Wp.14 118M) with good views down over the **Orotava Valley**.

Our route now climbs up around a spur in the valley wall and then undulates along before dropping down into a sharp ravine, crossing the ravine's two watercourses (Wps.15 & 16), our voices echoing in this beautiful orogenical landscape. We turn into another ravine, dropping down to cross its watercourse, then climbing out to come into a most unusual ravine with a 'rock boulder river' (Wp.17 130M) falling from the heights above us, steeply down the valley wall.

The steep valley of **Barranco de la Madre** widens out as we meander along a steady ascent, curving left to resume progress along the valley wall. A fallen pine is easily negotiated just before we zigzag up to a higher level to continue westwards (W). We continue ascending past a second fallen pine, the high altitude woodland and ravine path having some areas of unprotected drops, but not seriously vertiginous so far.

After swinging south (S), we drop down to cross another steep ravine (Wp.18) and another climb before our path starts descending through hairpin bends in lazy zigzags to bring us down to a rock viewpoint overlooking **Aguamansa** (Wp.19 155M).

From the *mirador* we continue downhill on the rock and shale surface to turn into a pocket in the valley wall where we come below a huge knob of rock. We cross the cutting's first watercourse by a pair of boulders and then cross the second watercourse directly beneath the huge knob of rock. Due to the mountainous landscape, we lose GPS coverage in this section of the route as our path climbs beneath steep cliffs. Now we have tree heathers on our right, creating a green tunnel effect until we come to face the vertiginous section. A rock ledge curves out of sight beneath overhanging cliffs (Wp.20), but don't worry. A securely fixed steel pipe provides a hand rail as we edge round into the unknown above a precipitous drop. Just round the corner we step off the ledge back onto a normal width path and regain GPS coverage for a short climb up to *mirador* viewpoint (Wp.21 170M) on a rock promontory; the guard rails referred to in some guidebooks rotted away over ten years ago!

There's still some climbing to be done, as our path undulates along the valley wall (poor GPS coverage in places), to climb out of the pine forest onto a ledge (Wp.22 184M, possibly vertiginous for some) with stunning views in good weather. Further on we pass a rock outcrop (Wp.23) providing another viewpoint over the valley before turning down into a ravine, the trees clearing again for more views, after which the path becomes a rough rocky descent of long lazy zigzags to cross a ravine's watercourse (Wp.24 202M). In the next ravine (Wp.25), three steep valleys meet, each stuffed with endemic trees and plants, unusual in this rocky landscape.

Views from Wp.22

Just past the ravine we lose GPS coverage as we come to face a long slope. Trudging up the steep incline, we finally arrive at the junction with our 'Chimoche Loop' route (Wp.26 215M) and can swing downhill on the grit trail to a path junction (Wp.27 222M).

You could continue straight down to **Lomo de los Brezos** but we're looking for a less skittery descent, so we go left at the junction to descend on a gentle woodland trail above a gentler valley, when compared to the orogenical landscape earlier. Coming to a junction, we take the lower path to the right which winds down through the woods, our path becoming more trench-like as we descend before we drop down onto a dirt *pista* (Wp.28 233M). **Lomo de los Brezos** is to the right as we go left to climb up to the junction at **Pasada de los Bestias** (Wp.29). Keeping straight ahead, we are on the *pista* which descends from **Choza Chimoche**, unremarkable except that we have a fast, easy walking descent through the forest down to cross the **Caldera** ring road (Wp.30 252M). Across the tarmac to follow the path through the woods, then we step down onto the end of the **La Caldera** car park (254M, actual walking time excluding breaks).

If you enjoy all-day walks on country lanes, then this is the route for you. We walk on good *pistas forestales* with our finishes on narrow *camino rural* tarmac lanes. Originally we finished in **Santa Ursula**, but not everyone wants to go to **Santa Ursula** so we have an alternative ending passing through **Pino Alto** to finish at **La Florida**. *Pistas* are technically public rights of way, but more locked gates are appearing on private dirt roads, which look exactly like *pistas forestales*. Private landowners are becoming much more protective of access to their land so that you could well find old walk descriptions of this region which use farm tracks and paths are now impassable.

Grab an early bus up to **La Caldera**, pack plenty of refreshment and wet weather gear in case the weather changes, and enjoy a grand tour of the forest and farmland which makes up the eastern **Orotava Valley**.

Access by bus: Service N°345 drops you off at **La Caldera**.

Starting from the **La Caldera** car park and bus stop (Wp.1 0M) we stroll out past the bar and onto the **Pista Monte del Pino**.

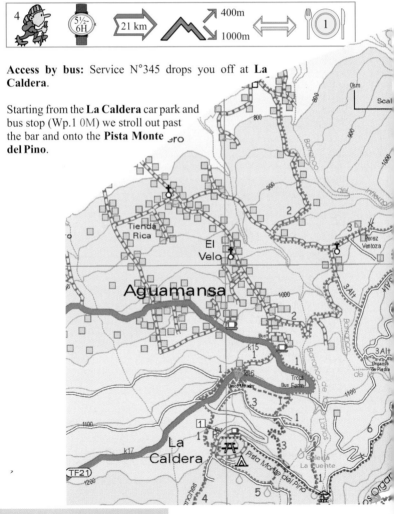

On the Monte del Piño 'motorway'

Keeping to this 'walking motorway' that we now know so well, we climb up to the **Choza El Topo** (Wp.2 45M) and its path and *pistas* junction. We continue straight ahead on the main *pista* to drop down and cross the **Barranco del Infierno** watercourse amongst lichen-bearded trees (Wp.3).

Now it is steadily uphill between the cliffs and the ravine to come up to the **Llano de los Corrales** plinth (Wp.4) and a path dropping down into the valley. Our route turns away from the steep *barranco* in a steady and seemingly relentless ascent, scaling the eastern valley wall in a series of hairpin bends. A large stone cairn (Wp.5) shows we are well into the climb with only two more major hairpins before we reach the crest (Wp.6) where the *pista* runs through a rock cutting.

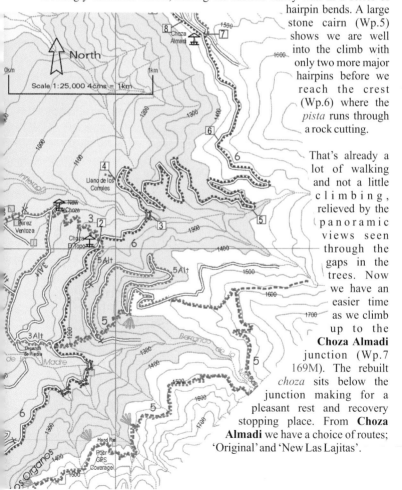

That's already a lot of walking and not a little c l i m b i n g, relieved by the p a n o r a m i c views seen through the gaps in the trees. Now we have an easier time as we climb up to the **Choza Almadi** junction (Wp.7 169M). The rebuilt *choza* sits below the junction making for a pleasant rest and recovery stopping place. From **Choza Almadi** we have a choice of routes; 'Original' and 'New Las Lajitas'.

Original DWG Route

Keeping to the main *pista*, signed to **Corujera** and **Santa Ursula**, we drop down (N) in a gentle descent through the forest with occasional yellow diamond *sendero* signs nailed to trees. A kilometre on, we come to the **Cruz de Tea** marker plinth where we ignore the *pista* going left into the valley and keep to the main *pista* to gently descend through the trees before a steeper descent brings us down to **Lomo del Barreno** marker plinth at a major junction of forest tracks. We keep straight ahead on the **Monte de Santa Ursula** *pista* to drop down past the municipal boundary 'T.M.La Orotava'. At the next junction, **Piedra del Agua** we continue on the main *pista* to come down to a major junction at **Los Assientos**, 'Carretera Dorsal' is off to the right and 'Morro Los Pinos' off to the left, while we cross straight over.

At the next junction, **Morro Los Pinos** and with 'Morro Los Pinos' signed on the forest track to the left, we again continue on the main *pista* signed for 'Pino Alto, Santa Ursula, La Orotava'; some of these forest tracks are as well signed as the main roads.

Gently descending, we pass an unsigned *pista* off to our left before arriving at **Montañas de las Ovejas** where 'Las Arenitas' is signed back the way we've come. Staying on the main *pista*, we come down to a junction at **Coral de Gabmorra**, and ignoring the 'sin salida' track, we continue down past the **Jueves de la Cueva** name marker, and a trail signed to 'Zona Recreativa', before we come down to join our new route. This is pleasant strolling route in good weather, but our new route from **Choza Almadi** is both more spectacular and shorter.

DWG Las Lajitas Route

At **Choza Almadi** we leave the **Pista Monte del Pino** by going left on the broad *pista* heading north west. Soon the track divides (Wp.8), going straight ahead on the smaller *pista* takes us up for views over the valley before

dropping down to rejoin the main track again (Wp.9). We drop down, passing minor *pistas* off to our right (Wps.10 & 11) before our route runs out onto a broad *lomo* at **Las Lajitas** (Wp.12) where, from the cross, we have one of the best views of the **Orotava Valley**. There's also an undamaged *choza* opposite the cross, so if **Choza Almadi** is occupied you could postpone lunch until reaching **Las Lajitas**.

Below **Las Lajitas**, a recently bulldozed *pista* has eliminated the paths referred to in some walking guides, confusing some walkers. We drop down this *pista*, very slippery if wet, to pass a minor track off to our right (Wp.13), then coming to another junction (Wp.14) where we go right. We have come down into one of the pockets of the original laurel forest (Wp.15) as we stroll beneath the dark green leaf canopy with rods of sunlight penetrating the thick woods.

As we emerge from the laurels we face a confusing T-junction (Wp.16) where **Pino Alto** is signed both left *and* right. We go right to cross the municipal boundary (Wp.17) and come to a T-junction (Wp.18 228M) where our original route joins us from the **Pino de las Nigeres** *pista* coming into the junction from the right.

We leave the junction on the **Hoya la Mora** *pista* for a gentle downhill stroll which brings us to the **Quatro Caminos** name marker (Wp.19) at another major *pista* crossroads.

Taking the one marked, 'Pino Alto, La Orotava, Santa Ursula', we continue down through the forest to the next junction (Wp.20) where a *pista* is signed left as 'Pista La Orotava'; don't believe this sign, as going left here would just take you back in a loop to the two 'Pino Alto' signs junction (Wp.16).

Keeping right, our route now curves right below the trees, with tree heather on our left, for us to come along to **Lomo el Canario** (Wp.21) and the junior sized shelter, table and benches signed 'Servicio Reten Incendio'. Our *pista* curves left, giving glimpses of farm land as we pass a donkey trail on our right (Wp.22) to come to views down over farm plots to the north coast with its breeze block townships.

Our *pista* turns sharp right (N Wp.23) with a minor track off to the left and we pass two more *pistas* off to our left (Wps.24 & 25) before coming down to **Las Charquitas** (Wp.26 277M) for a choice between **Santa Ursula** and **Pino Alto** routes.

Santa Ursula finish
At **Las Charquitas** we continue straight ahead onto the tarmac lane.This *camino rural* turns left and then heads directly down in a steep descent past farm plots and small settlements, starting at number Nº67 where the lane gets even steeper. A final very steep section drops us down onto a T-junction on **La Corujera's** 'main road'. We go left and first right to continue the steep descent past **Bar Casa Fefe**, taking the pedestrian street **Calle Los Quartos** as a short break from the traffic. It's all steeply down, taking a staired pedestrian path, before dropping onto the main road on the western outskirts of **Santa Ursula**. From here you could stroll into the centre of the town for refreshment, or wait at the first bus stop for the frequent bus service to **La Orotava** and **Puerto de la Cruz**.

Finish to La Florida via Pino Alto
At **Las Charquitas** we turn left onto the **Pista Rosade Aguila** which heads westwards. It's a rough, little used *pista* that steadily descends past a barred track on the left (Wp.27) before dropping more steeply to a T-junction (Wp.28).

We go right on a more comfortable surface, curving right to come onto tarmac by a house (Wp.29) just before a T-junction (Wp.30). Turning left, we simply stay on the main lane as it drops down the steep valley wall in a large zigzag before running out past **Pino Alto** church (Wp.31) to a T-junction (Wp.32 327M).

Going left, we have a skittery steep descent down past the houses of **Pino Alto**, the walking becoming easier as we leave the houses behind and cross the valley floor to face the climb up to the crossroads and 'urban choza' in **La Florida** (Wp.33). You could wait for the bus here, or go right and follow the street round **La Florida** and across the **Barranco de Quinquita** to climb up to the TF-21 with a wider choice of buses (370M).

A mountain walker might think it's the **Barranco del Infierno** above **Adeje** where pressure of numbers now means you have to book your walk. Possibly **Barranco de Masca**, beloved of guided walk organisers with a boat return to **Los Gigantes**, or perhaps **Siete Canadas**, (Walk 37) another guided walk favourite.

Think again. Tenerife's most popular walk is the sea front promenade/pavement that extends from **Costamar** apartments on the south-east outskirts of **Los Cristianos** heading around the coast, taking in all the beaches of **Los Cristianos**, **Playa de las Americas**, **San Eugenio**, **Torviscas**, **Playa Fañabe** and **Costa Adeje** before it finishes over ten kilometres later at **La Caleta**.

Geranium Walk dates back to 1988 when we were waiting for our BookSwop shop to be fitted out in **Puerto Colón** marina, at that time the western limit of the resort. Hardly anyone knew where **Puerto Colón** was, certainly not first time visitors, who seemed to be permanently lost throughout their holiday, so in the absence of any street plans we set out to produce the first **Las Americas/Los Cristianos** combined street plan - we walked all the streets and walkways to produce our first map. Then what better way to promote our business than to invent a walking route that finished at **Puerto Colón** overlooking the BookSwop. Published in September 1988, our new street plan was taken up by everyone while Geranium Walk appeared in the local English press as a 'spoof' walking adventure including such descriptions as 'scaling the Bouganville Alps'. We named the walk after the pink pelargoniums which lined the promenade between **Pueblo Canario** and **Puerto Colón**, the route featuring in our very first Tenerife South Walking Guide. So popular was this promenade adventure that when the authorities came to name the resort's streets, they used our street plan and 'Geranium Walk' became the official name for this coastal promenade.

Over two decades since its inception, Geranium Walk has been extended north-west as far as the traditional fishing village of **La Caleta** giving us over ten kilometres of promenading without ever having to cross a road. Much of its length has been upgraded and refurbished to provide a world class promenade.

All resort life is here; cafés and restaurants abound, shops offer everything from 'tourist tat' to full designer wear, beaches abound; plus if you don't fancy walking back from **La Caleta** you can always catch the frequent Titsa N°418 bus service back to the main areas of the resort. You can even use Geranium Walk to access our southern routes of Walk 7 Life in the Raw, Walk 8 Barren Grandeur, Walk 9 Mount Guaza and Walk 11 Picos Las Americas. So if you fancy a seaside promenade, look out your street shoes, take some pocket money for those ice creams to die for at **Sal y Tien**, and be ready to experience one of the world's great sea-front walking routes. For a street plan of your route and bus information see our Tenerife Bus & Touring Map.

This walk leaves tourism behind and heads off into countryside, providing an excellent introduction to the rugged southern landscapes. Our route begins in **La Caleta** and follows coastal paths, taking in the hippie colony at **Spaghetti Beach**, beaches and *barrancos* on our way to **El Puertito** for refreshments before returning.

Since we first walked this route, **La Caleta** has expanded from a little coastal village into the last outpost of the **Fañabe** tourist development complete with hotel, apartments and a more frequent bus service. Development has added an extra dimension to our route, making for a complete contrast between our start point and the wild country that lies beyond the first ridge, just six minutes away.

Access by car: La Caleta is north of **Playa de las Américas**, above **Costa Adeje**. There's a car park and on street car parking near the cross roads in **La Caleta** or on **Calle Les Artes**.

Access by bus: N°s 416 and 418 services to and from **Las Americas/Los Cristianos** approximately every 40 minutes.

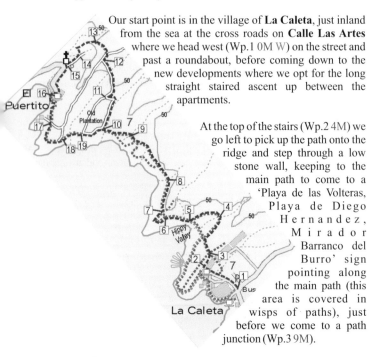

Our start point is in the village of **La Caleta**, just inland from the sea at the cross roads on **Calle Las Artes** where we head west (Wp.1 0M W) on the street and past a roundabout, before coming down to the new developments where we opt for the long straight staired ascent up between the apartments.

At the top of the stairs (Wp.2 4M) we go left to pick up the path onto the ridge and step through a low stone wall, keeping to the main path to come to a 'Playa de las Volteras, Playa de Diego Hernandez, Mirador Barranco del Burro' sign pointing along the main path (this area is covered in wisps of paths), just before we come to a path junction (Wp.3 9M).

Here we have a choice of routes into **Hippie Valley**; ahead is the steeper route, while we take the right hand option marked as suitable for wheelchairs!

Once named **Spaghetti Beach** in the days when an Italian naturist chef cooked here wearing only a sea captain's cap, this 'alternative' valley is dotted with hippie shacks of rock boulders and palm fronds, and tepees. The path runs around the valley giving us an arms' length view of their natural lifestyle, crossing the valley's watercourse on a stone-laid section (Wp.4), before it runs gently down to meet the shorter route (Wp.5 15M).

Hippie Valley

Our path climbs gently before starting a steep ascent of the valley's western wall. Just before the top of our climb a path goes left as we continue up to a junction of paths where we continue ahead to a *mirador* cairn set on the headland. From the *mirador* we head inland, meeting the paths from the top of the ascent (Wp.6) where we keep left to pick up the main path again (Wp.7 24M). Continuing ahead, we cross the high ground and begin dropping down into *barranco* country, waves breaking far below us as we descend on the well-made trail to more hippie encampments in the *barranco*. This large cove is formed by three *barrancos* meeting the sea, giving rise to interesting geological formations.

We cross the watercourse (Wp.8 27M), then climb gently uphill, staying on the main path and ignoring side paths off to camping areas. Over the headland between the two *barrancos*, our path is now stone over rock, heading towards long-abandoned plantations on the far side of the second *barranco*. We begin to drop into this second *barranco*, the path much less clear now until it crosses the watercourse (Wp.9 31M).

As we ascend we come onto a clearer path which meanders along to the remains of an old dirt road that becomes concrete as it climbs towards an abandoned plantation. The concrete ends on a spur and we drop into another small *barranco* before climbing rock sheets, up to a dirt road around the old plantation (Wp.10 42M).

Looking across to the towers of Playa Paraiso

We follow the dirt road inland, running up into a valley past abandoned terraces before becoming water-eroded as it curves up and round the sad terraces to the end of the plantation walls and a T-junction (Wp.11 46M).

Turning right, we follow the dirt road inland in a steady climb, the towers of **Playa Paraiso** coming into view, crossing the valley's watercourse and coming up to a T-junction (Wp.12 50M). We turn inland onto the more major dirt road for a few metres to find our path off left, crossing an old stone water channel, our path widening to almost dirt road width and curving into the *barranco* with **El Puertito** on our left.

The path swings left to an electricity pylon (Wp.13) and a path runs along the spur of bare rock before becoming indistinct. We continue down the spur to lose height before we need to leave the ridge and scramble down the rocks and stone slopes to meet an old dirt road at the back of the village (Wp.14 62M) which takes us to **El Puertito's** small church and parking area (Wp.15) where we step onto the tarmac road curving down onto the sea front of **El Puertito** and **Pepe y Lola's** little bar (Wp.16 70M).

After refreshment we begin our return (0M) by walking in front of the bar and following the path which wriggles between the jumble of houses to climb out of the bay and onto a headland where we pick up the coastal path. We cross a dirt road (Wp.17 5M) and continue on the coastal route, passing a *Espacio Natureleza Protegido* signpost with no board as we head towards the old plantation that we skirted on the outward route. Our route widens to a dirt road, taking us to the edge of the *barranco* (Wp.18) and onto a path which descends to its floor, crossing it on an old stone wall and climbing up towards the banana plantation on the next headland, heading towards its nearest corner where rock steps take us up to the level of the plantation and a dirt road (Wp.19 10M).

On the return

Following the dirt road right, we meet our outward route (Wp.10) and retrace our steps across the *barranco* before descending the concrete and dirt road.

Now it's simply a case of retracing our outward steps, possibly taking the steep short cut across **Hippie Valley** to arrive above **La Caleta**.

Here, if it's not windy, you could venture out along the point for the spectacular views into **Hippie Valley** seascape before descending to the village to seek refreshments.

Deserts and deserted coastlines have a beauty all their own. Here we have a linear route crossing the **Guaza Plateau** then dropping into **Palm Mar** before heading out along the deserted coast to **Faro de Rasca**. From the *faro* we continue along the coast to finish at the selection of restaurants on **Las Galletas** sea front, with a link to Walk 10, 'Coastal Escapism', if you want to continue on to **Los Abrigos**. Originally published as a circular route, we now include this option as an 'alternative finish' if you're looking for a 'desert & plateau' circular tour.

Quite a number of adventurous tourists tackle the path running up onto the **Guaza Plateau**, where, if without a guide book, they tend to follow the main paths over the plateau onto the main track, then descend to **Los Palos Golf** to face a hot road walk up to **Guaza**, from where there is the new road around the north of **Mount Guaza** back to **Los Cristianos -** a far from pleasant route with too much road walking alongside fast traffic to include as an 'official route', and certainly no match for 'Barren Grandeur'. The prize for the 'most lost tourists' must go to the three lads with towels over their shoulders that we met striding up the final track of **Mount Guaza** looking for 'the beach'!

** 4 on **Las Galletas** seafront, 1 in **Palm Mar***

Access by car: Follow the main dual carriageway of **Avenida de Los Cristianos** down to its roundabout to continue straight over passing the **Gran Arona** hotel on your right to a junction by the **Costamar** apartments. Continue straight ahead on the **Avenida Amsterdam** and after it swings left, start looking for an on-street parking place.

Access by bus: Take any bus to **Los Cristianos**, then follow the 'Access by Car' with the option of our alternative start from the **Costamar** apartments.

LOS CRISTIANOS TO PALM MAR

Alternative Start
From the **Costamar Apartments** at the southern end of **Los Cristianos** (0M), we follow the tarmac lane down to a walled villa to swing left and follow the beach path along to an *Espacio Naturaleza Protegido* sign where we climb up onto a path to start zigzagging up the cliffs - alternatively, walk along in front of new villas to new stone steps and climb up to the traditional route. Our well-marked path gets rougher as we climb, to join our 'official' route at a junction with a new path coming in from our left.

Official Start
Approx half way up the northern leg of **Avenida Amsterdam** a path drops into the water-runoff and up to a 'Protegido' sign (Wp.1 0M) we follow the path as it angles across the open land to join the old path (Wp.2 3M). Our path gets rougher, changing from dirt to broken rock as we climb up through a hairpin bend and keep steadily ascending until the route turns into a cleft (Wp.3 9M) approximately half way up the cliffs; if you look towards **Los Cristianos** at this point, you'll be facing directly towards the **Princesa Dacil Hotel**.

We take a faint path which climbs steeply away from the main walking route (SW) to pass a small cave. We're now climbing above our earlier route, and our path becomes more defined. Up through a hairpin bend (Wp.4), then another, we continue up onto the plateau to go over a crest and meander into a shallow valley to a T-junction with another path (Wp.5 23M). Heading right (SW), we follow the

path to a bald knoll (Wp.6), once a the *parapente* launch point, giving us beautiful views down onto **Los Cristianos** and inland to **Mount Teide**.

Beautiful views from the plateau

We go south-west on a path which drops into a *barranco*, where we cross its watercourse (Wp.7), then climb its southern side back up onto the plateau to curve around the cliffs before turning into a valley where our path contours round to cross the watercourse (Wp.8 33M), before bringing us back above the sea. Our path wanders through a landscape of tumbled valleys (SSW) which drop into the sea on our right until we meet a larger *barranco*. Small shale heaps show that this was once a stone-cutting area, as we head inland past a shattered rock before crossing the *barranco* floor (Wp.9 41M) and heading seawards; before reaching the sea our route swings left (S) into a small valley littered with shale heaps. Cresting a small rise, we see a large stone quarry on the far side of a valley; curving left, we descend into the valley and cross the stream bed (Wp.10 48M) below a second quarry.

Although the main path leads off to the further quarry, we look for a path on our left which climbs up alongside this quarry to become clearer when we are upon the plateau. Now it's easy strolling (SSE) past a path off to the left (Wp.11 44M) by the remains of a cairn, to the top of the cliffs overlooking **La Arenita** beach at **Palm Mar**. In a few metres we meet a path coming from the plateau on our left (Wp.12 48M), a cairn marking the start of the path's descent down the cliffs.

On the path, we go right and left past the substantial cairn to start descending the wall of a valley to a path junction (Wp.13) where a trail heads north back onto the plateau. From here we have an adventurous descent, and care is needed due to the loose stones which litter the generally well-made path. We wind down the wall of this sharp valley towards the beach, our route taking to bare rock where a section of path has fallen away. The path drops steeply down below a burnt orange rock outcrop for an almost scrambling descent before our route runs out into a tumbled landscape to a 'protegido' sign (Wp.14 73M). We swing down an old track to arrive on a dirt road which runs

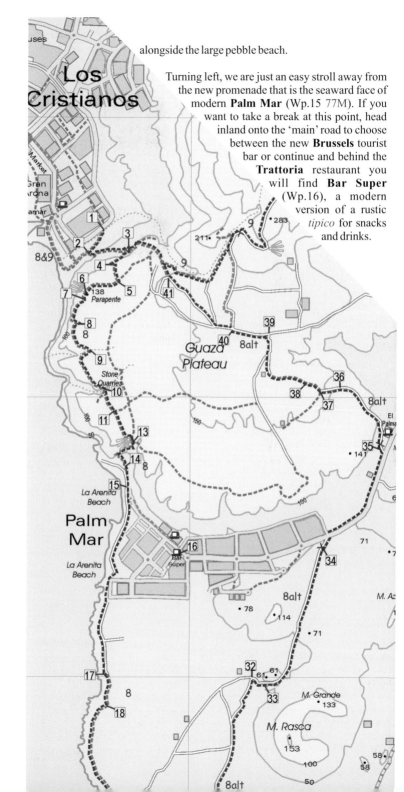

alongside the large pebble beach.

Turning left, we are just an easy stroll away from the new promenade that is the seaward face of modern **Palm Mar** (Wp.15 77M). If you want to take a break at this point, head inland onto the 'main' road to choose between the new **Brussels** tourist bar or continue and behind the **Trattoria** restaurant you will find **Bar Super** (Wp.16), a modern version of a rustic *tipico* for snacks and drinks.

On the seaward side of **Palm Mar** (0M) we stroll along its new but little-used promenade to come onto a road and up to a mock tower where we find a track heading towards the *faro*; the mock tower is an imaginatively designed sewage pumping station.

Our track undulates along to a large parking area (Wp.17 16M) where we take

A foaming inlet after Palm Mar

to a narrow walking trail winding its way amongst the lava foreshore to bring us onto a small flood plain. Across the sandy plain, we come through a tumbledown wall back onto the coastal path (Wp.18), faint at first but then gradually becoming more defined as we follow the line of the rocky coastline to come along to battered 'protegido' sign at the end of a stone track (Wp.19 36M). A boulder with a red bull's-eye marks our path's continuation through the *malpaís* past rock shelters and a pair of foaming inlets.

Across a sandy area, we continue amongst tumbled lava and over a ridge crowned with rock shelters which overlooks a pretty bay. Our route heads south-south west to crest another ridge, then comes to a junction overlooking another picturesque bay (Wp.20 49M). Now we head inland on a rough rock road onto a flood plain to head inland on a sandy path to a dirt track (Wp.21 56M).

Going left is our 'Alternative Return to Los Cristianos', while we turn right to cross a track junction and continue up to the *faro*'s access lane to reward ourselves with a break on the lighthouse steps (Wp.22 66M).

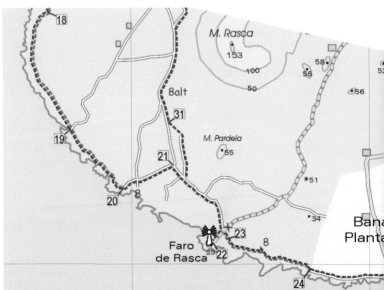

This route forms a section of our coastal route which links to **Las Galletas** and the start of our **Los Abrigos** route. This section starts well but becomes uninspiring, so look forward to the sea front restaurants!

Faro de Rasca

To the east of the *faro* is a huge covered banana plantation, and our first target is the seaward corner of this great tented structure. From **Faro de Rasca** we walk to the vehicle barrier on the tarmac lane and swing right (Wp.23 0M) down a rough sloping track.

From the bottom of the slope, a faint walking trail meanders eastwards (E) through the rocks, faint at times and with alternative paths but we keep generally heading for the plantation, before climbing up to a 'protegido' signpost (Wp.24 16M). at which point we drop down onto a broad dirt road on the seaward corner of the plantation

We stroll (E) between the massive foundations of the plantations and an impressive rocky coastline for over a kilometre, passing a tarmac plantation road before coming to the end of the dirt road and plantation (Wp.25 30M). We squeeze around a palm tree and boulder barrier to enter an area of *malpaís* where agriculture was abandoned decades ago.

A path takes us north-east alongside an old boulder wall; at its end (Wp.26 34M), we continue on a path heading for **El Fraile**. We pass the crumbling walls of old plantations to reach a cairn (Wp.27 39M) guiding us onto a trail which winds across the abandoned landscape, more cairns confirming our route. At a junction of tracks and trails (Wp.28 50M) yet another cairn guides

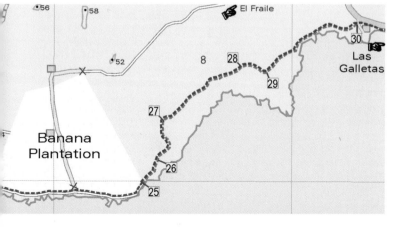

us along the trail heading towards **Las Galletas**, **El Fraile** now on our left. We take a well-defined path (Wp.29 53M) heading for the Red Cross 'Cruz Roja' building, passing small bays and wild camping before coming up to the Cruz Roja car park (Wp.30 66M). We now have an easy stroll along the pavement to **Las Galletas** for refreshments in one of the sea front restaurants.

LINK FROM LAS GALLETAS TO THE START OF WALK 10 'COASTAL ESCAPISM'

Walk east (E) through **Las Galletas** to come onto the main road heading north. Head inland, then turn off at the **Ten Bel Commercial Centre,** to walk east and then north to the **Chapparal Commercial Centre** with its totem poles. Continue east, passing **Chayofita** on your left and coming to the traffic island. From this point, choose either to go left then right, or right then left, to reach the alternative start points of our 'Coastal Escapism' route to **Los Abrigos**.

ALTERNATIVE FINISH - FARO DE RASCA TO LOS CRISTIANOS

Refreshed (0M), we retrace our route down into the *malpaís* until we come to the second dirt road junction where we go right (N). At the end of the dirt road where it turns back on itself (Wp.31), we cut across the open *malpaís* (NW) to strike a dirt road for us to head north. Passing dirt roads off to our left our dirt road curves around **Montaña Rasca** with a low stone wall on our right. It's easy strolling across the plain, passing more dirt roads off to our left before we come up to a T-junction (Wp.32).

Going right, we start climbing on the rough road to pass a 'pa' sign (Wp.33 25M) and continue ascending between red hills before curving left to cross a gentle plain ringed by small hills. Our road climbs gently up through a pass in the red hills to drop into a second plain with a fruit plantation away on our right. A second gentle climb through a second pass brings us to overlook the **Palm Mar** road and a gentle stroll down past the locked barrier (Wp.34 37M). We walk inland on the tarmac passing a walled bungalow, to just before **El Palmar** where we find an old dirt road marked by a 'pa' sign (Wp.35 47M) which climbs up onto the **Guaza Plateau**, the chain barrier by the 'pa' sign superfluous as the road has eroded to the stage of being impassable to vehicles. It's a hard slog up what remains of the road to climb above the restaurant and banana plantations as we curve towards the west

A large cairn (Wp.36) marks the end of the main climb as the gradient moderates to bring us up onto the plateau (Wp.37 63M). Here, by a small cairn, we step through a tumbled wall onto a walking trail lined with stones to come onto a dirt road (Wp.38). Our dirt road curves towards **Mount Guaza** (N) bringing us up to a T-junction below the farm (Wp.39) where we go left (W). When the main dirt road goes right (Wp.40) we continue straight ahead on a dirt road which curves round abandoned terraces. After descending gently, the dirt road swings left (Wp.41 82M) as we continue ahead on a walking trail to come onto the main path up from **Los Cristianos**. Once on the main path, it is all downhill - not that this is a relaxing section as the loose rocks littering the route demand care for every step. Halfway down the cliff face, we meet our outward route to retrace our steps back to **Avenida Amsterdam** or the **Costamar Apartments**, 105 minutes from **Faro de Rasca**.

Seen from the motorway, **Mount Guaza** appears inaccessible and so it is - but our route takes us up from the **Guaza Plateau** on an easy, but very strenuous, climb to the summit (428 metres). Being so close to **Los Cristianos** and 'because it's there', some people climb to the summit by accident; unbelievable once you've done it, but true - when we last walked **Mount Guaza** we met three guys with towels across their shoulders asking "Which way to the beach?" at waypoint 14! No refreshments on the route, though plenty when you get back to **Los Cristianos**.

Access by car: follow the main dual carriageway, **Avenida de Los Cristianos** to its roundabout and continue straight over, passing the **Gran Arona Hotel** on your right to a junction by the **Costamar Apartments**. Continue straight ahead on **Avenida Amsterdam**; after it swings left look for an on-street parking place.

Access by bus: any bus to **Los Cristianos**, then follow the 'Access by Car' with the option of our alternative start from the **Costamar Apartments** of Walk 8 to join our main route at Wp.2.

We start on the newish walking trail between the **Playa Graciosa** and **Paradise Park** developments on the edge of **Los Cristianos** (Wp.1 0M) by taking the steps down into the water runoff and setting off on the neatly manicured path for a gentle stroll up to join the traditional walking trail (Wp.2 3M). Turning uphill, we start climbing seriously through a zigzag, the path getting rougher while **Los Cristianos** gets smaller, then passing the turnoff of our **Palm Mar** route (Wp.3 8M).

On the climb from Los Cristianos

The going gets rougher as we come to a tempting path straight ahead (Wp.4 13M) but climb right on the main path. We keep ascending with our route swinging right to follow the *barranco*, passing paths off to our right (Wps.5 & 6) before coming to the junction (Wp.7 16M) with our return from **Faro de Rasca** route (Walk 3, 'Barren Grandeur').

We continue straight on - thankfully gradient free - beside an old water channel along the lip of the *barranco* until our path starts climbing up through the tumbled walls of old terraces (Wp.8) before returning to the *barranco*'s lip. There's more ascending through old terraces, including a section where the path splits in two (Wp.9) before rejoining, which brings us up to the end of an old dirt road (Wp.10 21M). We swing left to walk up a path facing the intimidating bulk of the mountain, the *barranco* dropping away on our left, to slog our way up to join the **Mount Guaza** dirt road (Wp.11 27M).

If you thought it was energetic so far - well, now it gets tougher as we slog up the wide and dusty dirt road, passing an old walking trail on our left before passing the vehicle barrier (Wp.12). The road swings right after the barrier to climb up to a hairpin bend with panoramic views, **Los Palos Golf** standing out like an emerald jewel amongst the dull, tented banana plantations. After a break for the views, it's back to slogging uphill, hills on our right and a *barranco* on our left, a seemingly endless ascent ahead on the dusty road. Cresting a rise (Wp.13 39M) we have a short section of downhill before the ascent is rejoined. Finally, the tops of aerials come into view as we walk up to a junction (Wp.14 56M) where a new dirt road sweeps left around the *caldera*. Straight ahead, we climb up the old road to pass a large cairn (Wp.15) and then a final steep slog brings us up to the trig point amongst the old transmitters (Wp.16 63M).

Technically, this is the top of our route - but not the end, as after a break to recover we continue down the old jeep trail (0M) to come down to the second set of transmitters (Wp.17) for views over **Playa de Las Américas**. Now it's easy strolling along the new dirt road and past the newest transmitters, then down to a junction (Wp.18) where we go out to a *parapente* launch point for views over **Los Cristianos** (Wp.19) and our start point way below us. Back on the dirt road, an easy stroll and gentle uphill bring us back to the junction with our outward route (Wp.14 20M). It's all downhill now (!) remembering to take as much care on the descent as the ascent, particularly on the very rough path down from the plateau, and we are back at our start point after 145 minutes, including a 17 minute break (to recover) at the trig point.

10 COASTAL ESCAPISM

This coastal walk is surprisingly interesting with its dramatic coastline and geology, quite in contrast to the boring landscape inland from our route. It's a good hike that works up an appetite for lunch in the **Los Abrigos** seafood restaurants, and is an ideal escape for those staying on either **Amarilla Golf** or **Golf del Sur** who can join the route as it follows the coast just south of each resort.

Dramatic coastline and geology en route

It's tougher than it looks on the map, although you can opt to finish the walk at **Los Abrigos**, in which case time and distance are approximately halved.

Access by bus: Routes N°s 467 & 470 link **Playa de Las Américas** and **Los Cristianos** with **Costa del Silencio**. Return from **Los Abrigos** on the 470 or 483.

Access by car: Park near **Coral Mar** or **Chasna** in **Costa del Silencio** (see start of the walk description below) and bus back on the N°470 if you want to finish at **Los Abrigos**.

Choose your starting point
Our start point in **Costa del Silencio** depends on the sea and wind conditions.

Rough sea start
If the sea is turbulent we start at **Coral Mar** (Wp.A1) and walk across to the *Espacio Naturaleza Protegido* sign to follow a clear path alongside a wall around the base of **Montaña Amarilla** which undulates gently along, passing a path off right (Wp.A2). We continue until we come just above a barrier to our left on a dirt road (Wp.A3), where we head downhill and seawards, passing a junction of dirt roads (Wp.A4) while looking for another *Espacio Naturaleza Protegido* sign down on our left (Wp.A5). This marks the 'official' path which we reach in the maze of dirt roads and paths in this confused area (Wp.8 12M).

Calm sea, low tide start
When the sea is quiet and at low tide we start off from the pebble beach below **Chasna**, to follow the shoreline around the rocks below **Montaña Amarilla**. We pass an *Espacio Naturaleza Protegido* sign and **Montaña Amarilla** on the left (Wp.1 4M), and begin to negotiate the rocks (popular with naturists at weekends and holidays, so watch where you put those boots), taking care as they are slippery.

The slippery rocks end (Wp.2 9M) and we climb a slope of rock to ascend onto the headland, where we find the coastal path (Wp.3 16M) which winds around between the impressive coastline and the *malpaís* inland, before dropping down to a 'pa' sign in a gully. Once on the official path, route finding is easy. We pass a junction of paths (Wp.4) where a staired route climbs **Montaña Amarilla** and another route goes left as we continue along the coast. A path runs off right to run around the headland (Wp.5 18M) as our walking trail meanders through this *malpaís* landscape with the rugged coastline on our right, passing another cross roads of paths (Wp.6 20M).

Now **Amarilla Golf, Golf del Sur** and **Los Abrigos** come into view ahead. A path runs back left towards **Montaña Amarilla** (Wp.7 24M) as we join our alternative starting point (Wp.8) near an *Espacio Naturaleza Protegido* sign.

Alternative, energetic start
Yet another start is to climb **Montaña Amarilla** (steeper than it looks, and dangerous if windy) to its summit and then follow the right hand path around the rim of the *caldera* before dropping down and heading seawards to pick up the coastal path.

The onward route
A dirt track comes in from the left (Wp.9 29M), and then vegetation begins, with *tabaiba* and prickly pear each side of the path (Wp.10 31M). Our path turns inland into a pebble dunes area (Wp.11 35M) with a pebble 'alps' inland, as we come down towards the bay of **Playa Colmenares**.

It's a wobbly walk across the pebbles to come onto a dirt road which drops us down behind the beach with a dirt road coming in from the left (Wp.12 44M). Following the road, or wobbly walking along the pebble beach, brings us to the end of the bay where we head between the sea and a lagoon to pick up the **Amarilla Golf** coastal path (Wp.13 47M).

This well-made path has the steepest ascents and descents of the whole route as it runs along the impressive coastline at the edge of the golf development. We pass a dirt road (Wp.14) which runs left into **Amarilla Golf** as we continue on the coastal path, passing the 5th tee (Wp.15) on the left. The path takes us

Looking back from Amarilla Golf coastal path

past apartments and a road off on our left (Wp.16 52M) and then a path left (Wp.17), which short cuts the ridge after waypoint 16 before running out at the entrance to the marina (Wp.18 64M).

After negotiating the marina bar we head east, and a path leads us up onto the black coastal walkway of **Golf del Sur** (Wp.19 67M), passing a walkway to the left (Wp.20) to stroll along past the **Santa Barbara** timeshare to follow the black path inland (Wp.21 72M) for us to come up to a road junction (Wp.22). Note: an alternative is to follow a well-walked path that follows the coast to arrive at Wp.24. We go right, turning onto **Calle San Miguel** and into **San Miguel** with **El Nautico** on our right (Wp.23) and taking a footpath onto the sea front walkway (Wp.24 80M).

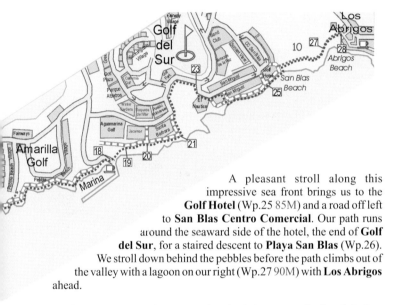

A pleasant stroll along this impressive sea front brings us to the **Golf Hotel** (Wp.25 85M) and a road off left to **San Blas Centro Comercial**. Our path runs around the seaward side of the hotel, the end of **Golf del Sur**, for a staired descent to **Playa San Blas** (Wp.26). We stroll down behind the pebbles before the path climbs out of the valley with a lagoon on our right (Wp.27 90M) with **Los Abrigos** ahead.

Across the headland, we have a semi-staired descent to the beach before ascending on a paved walkway to the edge of **Los Abrigos** (Wp.28 97M) which offers us a choice of bars and restaurants. If you'd prefer to ride back, regular bus services run between **Los Abrigos** and the resorts of **Costa del Silencio**, **Los Cristianos** and **Playa de las Américas**.

Our return to **Costa del Silencio** follows the same route, but as we approach **Montaña Amarilla** we have the alternative of following the base of the mountain on its inland (N) side. To take this alternative route, at the end of the dirt road leaving the *protegido* area marked by the signpost (Wp.A5) we begin to turn inland, passing a junction of dirt roads (Wp.A4).

Just before a gate across the dirt road we take an easy path which runs around the base of the mountain (Wp.A3), ignoring a path off left (Wp.A2) which runs into the *caldera*. As we enter the buildings of **Costa del Silencio**, we leave the path round the mountain near the **Chasna** building (Wp.A1) to walk the few metres (S) back to our start point.

The mountains in **Playa de las Américas** are on your doorstep - actually, your back doorstep, as our energetic but most rewarding route reveals. This route also links with the **TS-11**, giving options to continue on to **Adeje** (Walk 13, 'Adeje Skywalker') or to **Arona** (Walk 12, 'Down To Town'). This is our 'late afternoon training route' to try and keep in trim after a day working on our PCs, also serving as an introduction to exciting landscapes from an unlikely start location. The geology is memorable, but the demands of the final section make it suitable for experienced mountain walkers only.

3 | 1H | 3 km * | 350m / 350m | ⇔ | 0

* one way

Access by bus: numerous Titsa buses serve the CC San Eugenio bus stop a few metres from our start or walk back from **Playa de las Américas** bus station.

| **Short cut for car users** |
| Cut out the energetic climbs by driving up to the parking area at Wp.12. |

Town Section

Starting from the busy **San Eugenio** roundabout, we walk up the street with red metal palm trees on its corner, heading inland past the **Las Dalias Hotel** (Wp.1), to cross the motorway to a T-junction (Wp.2 5M). Going right, in 50 metres we turn onto a broad tiled path (Wp.3) to climb steeply up the broad stairway between the **Vista Mar** and **Roque Villas** developments, arriving breathless back on **Avenida Europa** (Wp.4). A steady uphill takes us onto **Calle Suecia** (Wp.5) and to another wide, steep and staired ascent (Wp.6) to emerge at the **Calle Portugal** junction (Wp.7 15M). Now it's onwards and upwards, ascending **Avenida Europa** to turn right (Wp.8) just before **Ocean View** for the last slog up to the ridge road (Wp.9 20M).

After the steep ascent, we are rewarded by an easy stroll towards the **Picos** (W) which are dramatically silhouetted against the bulk of **Roque del Conde** (Walk 20, 'Table Mountain'); unfortunately the seaward side has been ravaged by property development. There are sweeping views down over **Playa de las Américas** on our left and the banana-filled *caldera* on our right as we pass roads off to the left (Wps.10&11) to come to the parking area (Wp.12 25M). For the mountains section of the route, we take the times from the car parking area.

Picos Section

Due to the exposed

nature of the route, it should not be attempted in windy weather. From the end of the tarmac (Wp.13 0M), a track leads around a water tank before narrowing to a walking trail which used to climb steeply up to the 'pimple'; unfortunately the ugly development has stolen the original path meaning we have to edge along its fenced perimeter before joining the final section of path onto the 'pimple' (Wp.14 8M 305 metres).

The Picos Las Américas

After taking in the panoramic views, we stroll down to the saddle to begin ascending the first peak. Soon after the start of the climb, we need to swing left at a junction marked by a cairn (Wp.15) to continue steeply upwards. The path up to the first peak is not always clear, but if in doubt, climb up towards the highest point that you can see. The steep ascent eases as we come alongside the peak (Wp.16 14M), from which point a short scramble takes us up to the 358-metre high rock platform.

Back on the walking trail, our route becomes more difficult as we cross an old rock fall (Wp.17) to come onto a narrow, geologically remarkable rock ridge which leads to the second peak; the ridge is formed from two waves of molten lava crashing into each other and setting in that instant. Careful footwork and a head for heights are necessary in order to reach the basalt finger in front of the second peak (Wp.18).

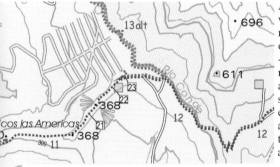

A narrow, sloping walking trail passes round the southern side of the peak (once again - careful footwork is needed), to bring us to another ridge; an easy stroll this time past an electricity pylon and across to the start of the third peak; (waymarks at Wps.19 & 20).

Our trail leads up in a steady climb to the small plateau at 368 metres altitude (Wp.21 35M) - now, that's what we call a panoramic view! We return by retracing our outward route to the tarmac road, and then the choice of descents into the resort.

Link to our Walks 12 'Down to Town' & 13 'Adeje Skywalker' routes
Once on the third peak we are close to our 'Down to Town' walking route. To link to Walk 12, continue along the ridge north-east (NE) to its end, again taking care with footwork. We then descend on its western side in an easy scramble to relatively flat ground. A faint trail with the remains of a stone wall on our right pushes through the undergrowth to bring us to an abandoned cottage (Wp.22). Beyond the cottage, a broad trail brings us onto the dirt *pista* of Walk 12 (Wp.23).

This walk follows one of the old donkey trails which link **Arona** and **Adeje**, although the old route has unfortunately been disrupted by high level developments in **Torviscas Alto**. For this eastern arm we have an easy country walk with impressive views, followed by the **Picos Las Américas** route for our descent into the resort - or in wet or windy weather, walk down through the new developments to finish in **Torviscas**.

Start with a relaxed ascent to **Arona** on the N°s 482 Titsa bus service.

Access by bus: N° 482 links **Arona** with **Los Cristianos**.

Extension
For a longer day out you can link to Walk 13, 'Adeje Skywalker' (in reverse) for a full transit between the south's 'county towns'.

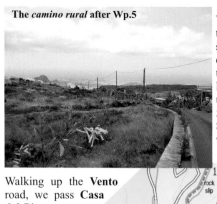

The *camino rural* after Wp.5

We start from the **Arona** bus terminus (Wp.1 0M) by strolling up the **Calle Duque de la Torre** paved street to the town square (Wp.2) and go left across the square to walk up the top road to cross the TF-51 onto the **Vento** road (Wp.3 8M), marked with a GR131 waypost.

Walking up the **Vento** road, we pass **Casa del Pintur** on our right before our route runs down to the Obelisk junction (Wp.4) in **Vento**.

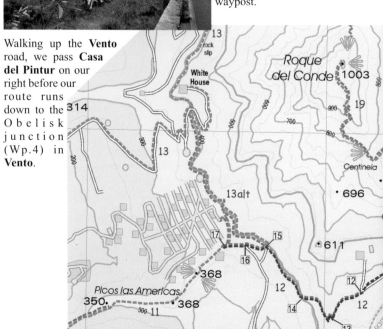

The sign at Wp.10

Going left, we pass the **Roque del Conde/GR131** route of Walks 19 & 20 (Wp.5 18M) just before going left on a *camino rural* tarmac road.

The narrow road drops down through abandoned terraces, passing an impressive house (Wp.6), before descending to a junction where another *camino rural* goes right across the *barranco* (Wp.7). After a short uphill houses line the road, then we drop steeply down to the TF-51 main road (Wp.8).

On the Camino Viejo de Adeje

Watching out for traffic, we turn right to walk down the road past the 3km marker to an old loop of the road (Wp.9) and on to the start of **Camino Viejo de Adeje** (Wp.10 38M) dirt road.

The dirt road sweeps us down to cross the watercourse of the first *barranco* (Wp.11), prickly pear and *tabaiba* dotting the *malpaís*. We climb up to pass an abandoned house on our left (Wp.12) before the cobbled trail zigzags down to

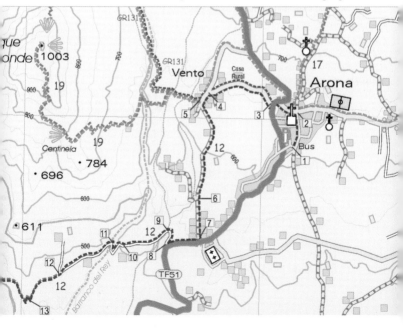

cross the **Barranco del Rey** (Wp.13).

Alongside the water channel at Wp.16

A steady climb brings us up to meet the friendly dogs of a neat-walled farm (**Wp.14 53M**). Passing the farm on our left, we stroll across the gentle slopes towards a low ridge which ends in a rocky outcrop. We pass a T-junction (**Wp.15**) where a dirt road goes right towards a white cottage, while we continue ahead on the water-eroded trail.

The condition of the trail improves as we stroll up to meet a water channel on the ridge (**Wp.16 60M**) from where we have spectacular views down over a *caldera* to **Los Cristianos** and **Playa de las Américas**.

This ridge might seem quite insignificant when seen from the east, but we face a steep descent on its west side, zigzagging down a donkey trail. The loose stone surface makes for a slow, skittery descent until we cross a broad working water canal (Wp.17 69M) known locally as the **Río Conde**.

Now we are on the gentle dirt path which runs alongside the **Río Conde** to give us an easy stroll along to a dirt road junction (**Wp.18**) where we turn downhill to a second junction (Wp.19).

The main dirt road runs down to the water treatment works on the floor of the *caldera*, while we go right on a fainter trail onto a saddle (**Wp.20**) between a water change point on the canal, and the **Picos las Américas** on our left (85M).

Onward routes: there are three alternatives:

A
Picos Las Américas Route
Go left (S) past the abandoned cottage to climb up onto the third peak of **Picos las Américas**, and follow this route across the exposed ridges (do not attempt in windy or wet weather) to the road system above **San Eugenio Alto** (30-40M), from where you have a choice of routes into the resort areas.

B
Go down into the development, and follow the roads down to the entrance of **Balcones del Conde** (15-20M).

C
Go up to the **Río Conde**, easiest from the first dirt road junction (**Wp.18**) and follow the canal above the development to meet our 'Adeje Skywalker' route. We then have options to descend to the **Fañabe** area or to continue on the **Adeje Skywalker** route to **Adeje**.

13 ADEJE SKYWALKER & THE WHITE HOUSE

This spectacular route is named for its awesome elevated views at almost every turn, giving the impression of being suspended above the southern landscapes - but it comes at a price. While most of the route involves easy walking on a paved water canal, the **Río Conde**, we have to cross an extremely vertiginous aqueduct and edge around a mountain above sheer drops; a good head for heights and sure-footedness are essential. There are also some sections where the paving is cracked or missing, requiring care. There's the option of a visit to **The White House** before finally heading down to **Playa de las Américas**.

*As an alternative to our 'expert' start from **Adeje** to the aqueduct, new development means that we can now drive up to the **Río Conde** canal on the highest **Torviscas** developments, offering the option for an easy stroll along the paved canal to southern Tenerife's very own 'White House'; see the walk description at the end of the main route description.

Access by bus: Adeje is a 'county' town with good services. Routes N°s 417 & 473 link **Los Cristianos/Playa de las Américas** with **Adeje**.

We start out from the bus stop by the top end of **Adeje** *cementerío* (cemetery), to go right in a few steps onto a dirt road (Wp.1), passing an archaeological sign for the **Grabados de Morro Grueso**, a protected site sacred to the Guanches, Tenerife's first settlers, whose 'graffiti' was found carved into the rocks.

The dirt road

Our dirt road winds down into the *barranco* to cross the water course (Wp.2), coming to a dirt cross roads where we go straight over to walk up the higher dirt road, passing through a metal gate (Wp.3) as we climb up onto the ridge at a U-bend (Wp.4 12M). Now the dirt road heads up the line of the ridge, passing a white cottage on our right and coming up to a junction just past a water tank (Wp.5 20M).

Water pipes cross our route as we continue straight ahead on the dirt road towards the mountains. As we gain height and the road becomes rougher, we pass *Naturaleza* signs (Wp.6) until we come to a faint path marked by a cairn (Wp.7 30M) where the rough dirt road swings west.

Taking the narrow path, we continue our steady ascent (NE) through the

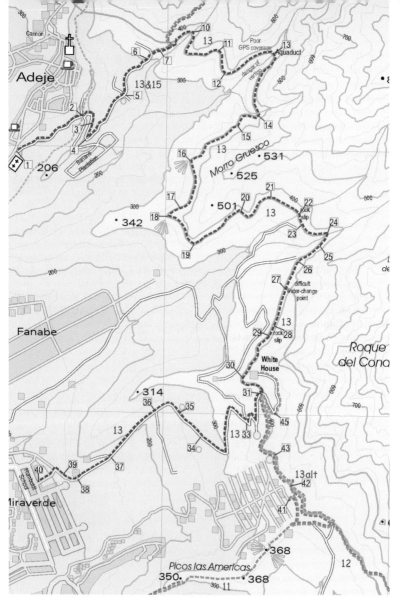

shrub-covered slopes, passing a small cairn (Wp.8), our path becoming fainter as we gradually close with the canal. Finally we clamber up onto the canal (Wp.9) for a relaxing break after the long ascent of slogging up dirt roads and narrow paths. We're on a broad paved water canal approximately 1 metre in width, which gives us an elevated walkway with sensational views - surprisingly, unknown to other walking writers. It's an easy walking surface, but take care to 'look where you walk, and STOP to look at the views', as there is no protection from the drops alongside the canal. An easy stroll takes us over a small bridge (Wp.10) before we curve round into a smaller *barranco* to cross its water course on another bridge (Wp.11 50M), then step out to a viewpoint (Wp.12). As the canal turns into the next *barranco* it becomes vertiginous, with sheer drops on our right and a cliff on our left causing poor GPS coverage. If you have any doubts over this section, return towards **Adeje**. We approach the major obstacle on our route, an aqueduct (Wp.13) which carries the canal over the steep **Barranco del Agua**, which drops down from **Roque Abinque.**

On the paved canal

In this dramatic orogenic setting of soaring mountains, cliffs and sheer *barrancos*, we edge over the thirty foot span, to a well-deserved rest at its eastern end (60M). After recovering from the aqueduct crossing, we soon face another vertiginous section where the canal runs under a cliff and there are some missing slabs; here we step onto the black water pipe to carefully negotiate these sections. Turning out of the main **Barranco del Agua** ravine, we cross a small bridge **(Wp.14)** to enter a landscape of gentler slopes. After another bridge (Wp.15) we walk out to a *mirador* view (Wp.16 78M) as the **Río Conde** swings left. A steel water pipe crosses the canal (Wp.17), just before we cross the **Morro Grueso** ridge (Wp.18) to swing above the **Fañabe** valley. We curve left (Wp.19) to see the **Río Conde** sweeping around the broad valley ahead of us.

Easy strolling takes us past a small cave (Wp.20 95M) and over a small bridge (Wp.21), before we come to a section where rocks and earth cover the canal (Wp.22). Picking our way over the rock, we come back onto the paved canal to pass a dirt road on our right (Wp.23) and cross a small bridge (Wp.24) before coming to a water change point (Wp.25 110M) where we drop down onto a dirt road which runs alongside the canal. We follow the dirt road until it swings right to drop into the valley (Wp.26) where we clamber back onto the paved canal. After crossing a bridge and a small canal which crosses the **Río Conde**, we come to a difficult water change point (Wp.27).

Some nimble footwork is needed to negotiate the inland scrub and change point to get back onto the paved canal. We stroll on, the dirt road alongside the canal turning away towards an abandoned cottage on the saddle between two valleys (Wp.28), then we climb over a small rock slip (Wp.29), taking care where there are occasional missing slabs before we're below the 'White House' which sits above water change points which are numbered 195-9 and 194-8 (Wp.30 124M). In a couple of minutes the canal passes underground and is crossed by means of the rough dirt access road to the 'White House' (Wp.31) which gives us the choice of an uphill diversion to one of the region's most noticeable but least visited landmarks - see the 'Alternative for Car Drivers' at the end of this walk description. Also see 'Alternative Finishes'.

Now we leave the **Río Conde** to head down the rough dirt road past a large water tank on our left (Wp.32), to a junction of dirt roads (Wp.33 140M) signed 'TS11' on our right. The dirt road is littered with shale and scree, making for slow skittery progress down past water tanks; those to the left **(**Wp.34**)** old and empty, and new and fenced to the right **(**Wp.35**),** before the dirt road heads straight down the side of the valley. Our walking surface improves as we pass dirt roads, to the left (Wp.36) and on the right (Wp.37), before we reach the first house and a tarmac lane (Wp.38 165M) to stroll down past the impressive entrance to **Finca Amapola de Fañabe** (Wp.39), then come onto the new road system behind the **Humbolt School** (Wp.40 170M).

Alternative Finishes
Alternative finishes involve continuing on the **Río Conde** to the new developments and then heading down to **Torviscas Alto** on the new road system, or continuing past the new developments to join up with the eastern arm of the TS-11 to follow the **Picos Las Américas** route down into the resort

*ALTERNATIVE FOR CAR DRIVERS: FROM TORVISCAS ALTO TO THE WHITE HOUSE

2/3 | 70M | 4.5 km | 100m / 100m | 0

From the **Torviscas/Playa Fañabe** motorway junction head inland up past **Villa Tagoro** on **Calle Galicia** to drive through the impressive arched entrance into the 'Roque del Conde' developments, still on **Calle Galicia**. Negotiate your way up, turning left at **Supermarket El Conde**, to the highest cul-de-sac to park (Wp.41) just below the saddle and cottage that feature in Walk 11, 'Picos Las Américas', and Walk 12, 'Down to Town'.

A clear path climbs up towards a gurgling water point on the canal, then levels out below the **Río Conde** to a viaduct over a water run off (Wp.42 5M) where we face a scrambling ascent alongside a water pipe to cross the canal onto a path that takes us over the run off on a wooden bridge before coming back to the canal. At a water point (Wp.43), there's a small diversion before concrete stairs take us back to the canal path, passing two more water points; the path is little walked and surprisingly floriferous making secateurs useful.

As **The White House** looms over us, the path takes us down to join its access track (Wp.44 24M). We turn up the access track to cross the **Río Conde** for a steady ascent up the rough jeep track, getting rougher as it heads away from our objective before swinging back (Wp.45) for us to trudge up to **The White House** (Wp.46 36M).

Our objective; The White House

After enjoying the elevated views from the pumping station, you could opt to continue along the **Río Conde**, easy walking until you approach the aqueduct, enjoying this unusual perspective of the resort areas along the coast. Otherwise, we return by retracing our route.

14 TAUCHO TOUR

A circular walk with a surprise finish - sounds improbable, but for our Taucho Tour, it's true. This is an easy route on old donkey trails taking in spectacular views, with excellent flora including an unusual floral phenomenon.

After a rather unpromising start the landscape exudes bucolic charm; in short, it's idyllic walking country and with a classic *tipico* (**Bar Taucho**) not far away.

Access by car: We start by driving west on the TF1 motorway and continue past the **Adeje** roundabout onto the TF82 and look for a right turning (easily missed) onto the TF583 road to **Taucho**.

After the twisting third gear ascent, follow the narrow road through the village (past **Bar Taucho**) and continue on the narrow lane (*camino rural*) as it drops into and climbs out of a barranco until we come to a church on our left and a parking area at **La Quinta**. Despite the bus terminus, TITSA's timetable does not include any services to the village!

From the corner of the church square (Wp.1 0M) we stroll along **Calle La Serrería** before leaving it in approximately 50 metres to go right (Wp.2) onto a smaller *camino rural*. Down into a small valley, the tarmac goes left to houses as we step right onto a broad dirt road (Wp.3) to continue (S) past large steel gates (Wp.4).

Just after the gates a dirt *pista* goes left, while we stay on the main dirt road which runs along to swing into a floriferous valley with a walking trail crossing the valley below us. We cross the valley's water course (Wp.5) to come gently uphill and meet the walking trail just before some steel gates.

Going left (Wp.6), we clamber up over rock to come onto the donkey trail's continuation as it skirts a fenced area, passing gates and an *embalse* (Wp.7), to come onto another dirt road. Shortly we take a walking trail off to the right (Wp.8) alongside a small *barranco*, which soon curves right to cross its floor (Wp.9), then brings us onto a dirt road that arrives from the left (Wp.10).

We swing along to a *parapente* launch point (Wp.11), with a most unusual official sign, to continue on a walking trail dropping into a steeper *barranco*. Across the watercourse (Wp.12), we climb up the southern wall, crossing a side *barranco* (Wp.13) for a final ascent to **Lomo de las Lajas** (Wp.14 28M), with its impressive

At Lomo de las Lajas

views to the south over **Adeje** and the coast.

Leaving **Lomo de las Lajas**, we go east to pick up the eroded walking trail which climbs steadily and curves left (this is part of our Walk 16 'Queen Of The South' route in reverse - and if you want really spectacular views go right to the top of the small ridge, but take care).

Impressive views from Lomo de Las Lajas

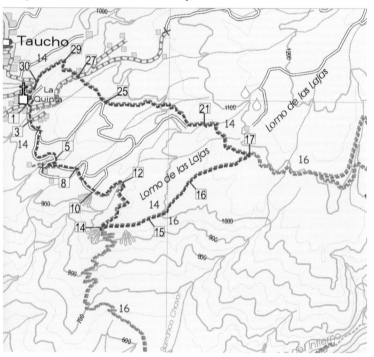

Our eroded trail brings us up to a gentle open ridge (Wp.15) ahead of us, then a path takes us up the left side of the ridge in a steady climb (the 'Queen Of The South' route is a few metres to our right), crossing a rock section (Wp.16) before coming onto the 'Queen Of The South' route.

Continuing the steady climb, we come amongst the pines on a well defined path to reach a junction (Wp.17 47M) where we go left, passing a large green dot to climb up to an 'Ifonche' route sign on the crest of the ridge (Wp.18) with its carved water channels.

Green dots guide us (W) on a faint path which zigzags down to the floor of the small valley (Wp.19), an old cottage above us on our right, then gently climbs up to cross a small ridge where we meet a steel water pipe (Wp.20).

Now our path follows the water pipe steeply down into this unusual *barranco*, its floor completely choked with brambles which stretch as far as we can see in a great green swathe that we've not seen anywhere else. We zigzag down before following the southern side to cross the watercourse (Wp.21 58M), at a cutting through the brambles, before climbing up over an old water canal to ascend the northern side still accompanied by the water pipe.

As we climb and move away from the valley, the bramble-choked watercourse is even more impressive until we turn away (Wp.22) to drop into another valley to cross its watercourse just below a mature pine (Wp.23), before a steady climb up for our path to cross open ground (Wp.24).

There are houses ahead of us as we descend alongside the pipe into another small valley (Wp.25) and climb up the path to cross open ground and into a minor valley (Wp.26) before climbing up the rough stone trail between stone walls to reach a *camino rural* (Wp.27) opposite a pair of houses. From here you could shortcut down the *camino rural* to the church, but we'll go for a surprise finish.

Across the *camino rural*, the water pipe continues past the fence of house Nº21 with its noisy dog. At first this looks an unlikely route but as we drop down, the donkey trail emerges for us to descend steeply down its boulder-laid surface into the **Barranco de la Quinta**. Zigzags bring us steeply down, taking care on the slippery pine needles by a mature pine (Wp.28), to come onto the valley floor (Wp.29) at the bottom of the sheer-sided *barranco*.

Green dots indicate a narrow path down the *barranco* floor, the rough boulders giving way to an easier surface before we emerge onto tarmac between **Taucho** and **La Quinta** (Wp.30). Ignoring a green arrow, we go left on the tarmac for a few metres to the start of a stone-laid trail (Wp.31) with a wooden handrail.

The trail starts steeply and gets steeper as it zigzags up the *barranco* wall; far too steep for a safe descent. Puffing and panting, we come up to the back of a white cottage for the final climb up onto a dirt road where our start point is a few metres away on our right (93M) - now, isn't that better than an easy finish?

Our original 'Wow! Spectacular' route appeared in '35 Tenerife Walks' and covered a small part of the **Camino Currasca** donkey trail linking **Ifonche** with **Adeje**, and was designed as an 'out and back' route from **Bar Dornajo** in **Ifonche** for car drivers.

Now we give you the full route in all its spectacular glory, and it certainly is spectacular; it's the most exciting mountain descent in the south of Tenerife, though this comes at the price of it being a tricky, picky trail, vertiginous in places, only suitable for experienced walkers in good weather. All the worst parts of the trail come after the end of our original 'Wow! Spectacular' route so you can use this as your decision point for whether to continue on the full route.

The mountain scenery and views are magnificent, so if you have the ability and good weather, this is an unforgettable route.

* but if walked later in the day, there are three bars likely to be open on the first section, plus choices in **Adeje** at any time.

Access by bus: N°342 from **Playa de Las Américas** and **Los Cristianos**, N°482 from **Los Cristianos**. Ask for **Cruce de Ifonche**, the next stop after **Casa Camillo** restaurant; some visitors call that stop 'La Escalona' but this is actually a few hundred metres further up the TF-51.

Access by car: linear route not suited to car access.

Riding up on the N°342/482 is a relaxing way to start an adventure and after our bus finishes its twisty climb above **Arona** to pass **Casa Camillo** we press the 'Stop requested' button; the driver will stop at **Cruce de Ifonche** junction (Wp.1 0M) for us to alight.

We set off up the **Ifonche** road (N) to swing over the *barranco*'s stone bridge for a second climb up to a crest of the road, giving views over the plateau ahead. As the narrow road sweeps down we pass the green bar on our right (unlikely to be open at this time in the morning) for an easy stroll across the landscape dotted with *fincas* while ahead, the peaks of **Imonde** and **Brezos** mark the plateau's southern limits.

Past **Bar Tasca Teguara** we come to the lonely *ermita* (Wp.2 20M) with a potable water tap and a dirt track signed for **Vilaflor**. Next is the **El Refugio** restaurant track junction to the left (Wp.3 27M) and we're now sharing the road with our Walk 19, 'Fantasia' route. After undulating across the plateau our road drops into the **Barranco del Agua** followed by a steep climb up to the tarmac crossroads at **El Dornajo** (Wp.4 41M); unfortunately also likely to be shut until lunchtime, though it does have a €1 cold drinks machine outside.

Straight over the crossroads, we continue on the tarmac lane for 120 metres

before turning right onto a track (Wp.5) to walk up to a waypost, 'Ifonche Casa Fuerte Adeje 9,500m 4.5 hours', which refers to our Walk 16, 'Queen of the South' route.

We take the signed path to wind through two small valleys amongst pine dotted slopes. Coming over a red earth spur, our trail drops down past old terraces towards an isolated cottage to meet a dirt road (Wp.6 57M).

Deep, isn't it?

Here our Walk 16 continues ahead, while today we go left, signed 'La Vista', to walk up past **Casa Nebraska** to a large threshing circle enjoying the spectacular *mirador* viewpoint of **La Vista** above the **Barranco del Infierno** - deep, isn't it?

From the threshing circle we continue along the track until it swings left for us to continue on a path which comes to the lip of the barranco (Wp.7 64M); we're now on the **Camino Currasca**.

On the narrow ledge

Our stone-laid donkey trail drops steeply, you could almost say 'plunges' - but best not to, down the *barranco* wall through the remains of a gate into an amazing pocket of flora. Here on a narrow ledge running under sheer cliffs, and watered by the trade winds driven up the ravine, are some of the best examples of Tenerife's endemic plant life.

It's a narrow path requiring careful footwork at times as we pass below the cliffs before ascending onto a saddle of sand-gold rock (Wp.8 82M) between the cliffs outcrop and **Roque Abinque**.

On the sand-gold saddle

This is a good place to take a break, enjoying these impressive views before tackling the difficult section of the route. From the east side of the saddle we take a small cairned path running along above the **Barranco del Agua**, ahead **Playa de Las Américas** is framed by the *barranco* walls, and a rock 'finger' indicates our next destination.

At a junction we keep left, the path right simply climbing to a stone corral, our path coming above an old water canal which we drop down to meet while running out towards the 'finger'

Our path now follows the canal, an eroded section requiring us to edge along the canal itself, to bring us to a right turn beside the 'rock football' topped 'finger' (Wp.9 95M) where a section of the old canal provides a gallery seat for us to look down through the orogenical landscape onto **Adeje**.

The rock football

Our original 'Wow! Spectacular' route finishes here. Looking right you can see why, as the path has fallen away! This means that onward progress must be across a section of the narrow old canal where a protruding rock threatens to tip you over the abyss, admittedly not an

The path after Wp.9

extreme drop, but still a drop to trigger the vertigo. (I got across so it can't be that bad! - David.)

This is quite the worst hazard on the **Camino Currasca**, sections after this are merely 'tricky', and we'll understand if you turn back at this point; not that your day is lost because you have the choice of

returning to Walk 16, 'Queen of the South' for the conventional descent to **Adeje**, or back to **El Dornajo** for Walk 19, 'Fantasia' with the option to finish in **Arona**, both of which have bus services to take you home.

... another spectacular panorama ...

Across the vertiginous canal section, our narrow trail now twists steeply down into the *barranco* to pass under cliffs and striations of orange rock on a picky descent due to loose rock on the trail, to 'red rock' corner (Wp.10). It's another spectacular panorama overlooking **Adeje**, this time including the **Río Conde** and its vertiginous aqueduct experienced on our Walk 13, 'Adeje Skywalker'.

Taking advantage of the seat-like rocks

On the next section we have a couple of landslips that require careful edging across, that's in addition to the loose rocks on the trail and intrusive shrubbery before we arrive at 'candelabra spurge' corner (Wp.11 120M) with its seat-like rocks.

Now we're amongst steep slopes rather than the sheer cliffs of earlier, with a stone laid trail to zigzag down over a ridge, bringing **Adeje** and the **Río Conde** back into view.

At another natural *mirador* (Wp.12 140M) we take a break; it's a long way down requiring concentration on the rock-littered path, so best to take breaks following our maxim of, 'Stop to look at the view, and look where you're walking'.

We continue down the stone-littered, picky descent with its intrusive shrubs, until a small ascent takes us into a side valley, our trail running along to cross the watercourse (Wp.13) before we turn back towards **Adeje**. If anything the rock litter gets worse, requiring concentration for every step, as we slowly edge downwards to come onto the **Río Conde** canal (Wp.14).

Taking the **Adeje** path with the green and white waymarks, we are on another picky descent to a jeep track (Wp.15), a junction easily missed if walked as an ascent.

Lush, endemic plant life

The jeep track is little better than the path, somewhat alleviated by the lush endemic plant life, until we come onto a dirt road (Wp.16) by a square *embalse* and at last we have a decent walking surface on which to head down into the *barranco*. A final uphill slog brings us up to the road alongside the cemetery (Wp.17 225M).

The nearest bus stop is downhill opposite the sports centre, while the closest refreshments are a hundred metres uphill, towards the town centre.

This walk certainly lives up to its royal title. We start at the **Ifonche** junction and set out on a journey through a 'timescape' of agricultural settlements, pine forests, incredible *barrancos* and valleys, to emerge at the best *mirador* view in the south. The final descent of 650 metres altitude into **Adeje** is unfortunately more memorable for the rough track than the views - good footwear is essential - but don't let this put you off this grand walk.

Alternative start	
An alternative but much tougher start can be made from **Arona**, by either walking up the **Vilaflor** road to the **Granja Arona** where we take the track down to the *embalse* in Walk 18 to follow its return route to **Ifonche**, or take the **GR131** Walk 20 in reverse from **Arona** through **Vento** to **Ifonche**, much more scenic but tougher and longer.	**Access by bus:** N°342 from **Playa de Las Américas/Los Cristianos**, N°482 from **Los Cristianos**. Ask for **Cruce de Ifonche**, the next stop after **Casa Camillo** restaurant; some visitors call this stop 'La Escalona' but that is further up the TF-51 on the route of Walk 17. **Access by car:** linear route not suited to car access.

From the bus stop at **Cruce de Ifonche** we walk up the road (N, see the first map for Walk 15, 'Wow! Spectacular to Adeje') before dropping down to cross the **Barranco de Funes**. A stiff climb then brings us up onto the **Ifonche** plateau, followed by gentle strolling along the road past two bars, the tiny church and the **El Refugio** turning, before going down into the **Barranco del Rey**. Another stiff climb then brings us up to the tarmac crossroads at **Bar El Dornajo** in **Ifonche**, sadly unlikely to be open before 13.00 (Wp.1 60M).

At **Bar El Dornajo** (Wp.1 0M) Walks 18 & 20 (combined route) go left, but today we follow the start of Walk 15, 'Wow! Spectacular to Adeje' route (Wps.2, 3 & 4), until we come down to the dirt road in the bottom of the valley (Wp.5 12M) where we head straight across the dirt road. Our narrow walking trail climbs up from the valley floor and turns inland to steadily ascend the ridge, bringing us up to a bowl where terraces have been built amongst the pines, or perhaps where pines have colonised former agricultural terraces. We come to the end of a terrace wall, the trail continuing below the wall and climbing gently to bring us to the edge of the pine forest (Wp.6 17M).

Near the start after El Dornajo

A clear trail leads into the forest, signed by a white arrow on a boulder, takes us gently uphill beneath the trees. We come up to a junction where we take the

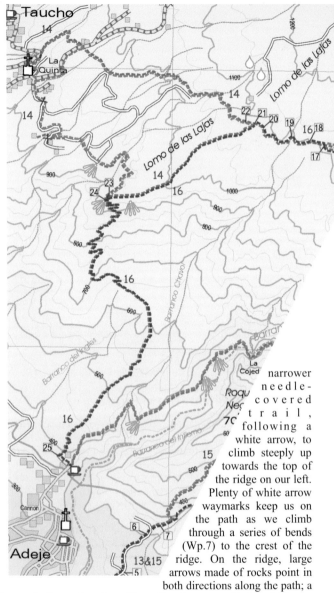

narrower needle-covered trail, following a white arrow, to climb steeply up towards the top of the ridge on our left. Plenty of white arrow waymarks keep us on the path as we climb through a series of bends (Wp.7) to the crest of the ridge. On the ridge, large arrows made of rocks point in both directions along the path; a small cairn marks the continuation of the path and we go gently downhill.

On our left we look down into the canyon of **Barranco del Infierno** and catch glimpses of the sea through the pines. Our trail runs downhill, with occasional climbs, along the wall of this magnificent canyon 250 metres above the route of the 'Barranco del Infierno' walk (see the appendices in the back of this book for details). We walk below sheer cliffs, the long drop into the canyon on our left as we progress towards the head of the *barranco*. The pine needle-covered path drops steeply, requiring care on the slippery surface, before levelling out to run below an impressive promontory.

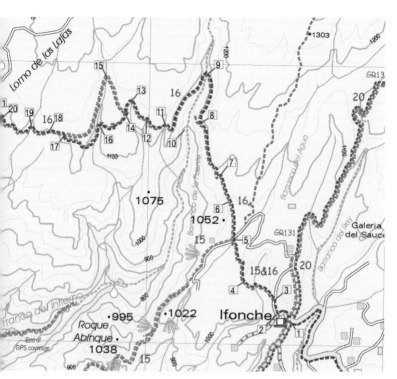

Sounds of running water and the waterfall come up from the canyon's depths, and passing through a rock channel, we go downhill to round a pocket in the canyon wall. The path runs down and out of the pocket to round a promontory by a mature Canarian pine; from here we enjoy *mirador* views down into the sheer-sided *barranco*. After the viewing point we come to a junction of paths (Wp.8 28M). We take the right hand path, signed 'TS3', to climb steeply up the narrow trail along the *barranco* wall. The path zigzags up to come under cliffs as we continue through a rock channel, and then more cliffs before the ascent eases. We now stroll along to an area where the tumbled boulders of a huge rock slide cover the steep slopes. Our trail cuts through the sea of boulders to drop steeply down until we come out onto the floor of the canyon (Wp.9 38M), now above the **Barranco del Infierno** and technically on the floor of **Barranco de la Fuente**.

Picking our way over the grey boulders, we come back onto the continuation of our route and start climbing up the western wall of the canyon. It's a stiff ascent on the steep rocky trail, increasingly pine needle-covered as we climb before the path levels out and we come under a large boulder. Our route undulates along the *barranco* wall before taking another climb. Pacing ourselves for the stiff ascent and taking rests when necessary, we toil up to come above the canyon (Wp.10). Looking back across the *barranco* we can see that we've climbed back up to a similar altitude to the trail's start at **Ifonche**.

After the exertions of climbing out of the **Barranco de la Fuente** we might hope for some gentle downhill walking. However, the trail leaves the views behind and takes us into a rather sombre section of pine forest which clothes a land of valleys and rugged *barrancos*. Our trail is clearly way marked with white dots and arrows as we cross gentle valleys (Wp.11) and two sharp-sided *barrancos* (Wps.12 & 13) beneath the shade of the silent forest. A few cistus 'rock rose' bushes relieve the tedium of this brown needle-covered ground. As the valleys become shallower we need to pay careful attention to the route's way marking.

Coming up a gentle slope we approach a pair of pines where the main path turns right (Wp.14 56M); looking to our right we see an arrow twenty metres up the gentle slope. Although this appears to be a major junction, both paths arrive at the same destination, the right hand path crossing **Barranco Chavon** at Wp.15 while the straight-on path crosses it at Wp.16 then, after climbing out of the *barranco*, runs on through the pines to a multi-junction of paths (Wp.17 72M) where we join the upper crossing route. Now the forest becomes more colourful as the trail leads us through a series of shallow valleys (Wps.18, 19 & 20) to a junction at the edge of the forest (Wp.21 88M). Ahead, the main trail leads up onto an area of clear rock with a signboard (Wp.22), the main route to **Taucho**.

Following the left hand trail, we come onto bare rock to find a hand-carved rock water channel. Boots have worn faint trails across the rock for us to parallel the small water channel. Away on our right we look over a *barranco* to the outlying houses of **Taucho** village, as our path continues going gently downhill to an area of red earth marked by a cairn. If you go over to your left at this point you will find the water channel again, and a spectacular view down over **Adeje** from the edge of the *cumbre*.

Panoramic views from Lomo de Las Lajas

This path swings right to run along below a low ridge and becomes badly water-eroded before it meets a path (Wp.23) and then swings left onto the donkey trail at **Lomo de las Lajas** (Wp.24 107M) with its superb panoramic views. The descent from **Lomo de las Lajas** starts well on a stone-laid donkey trail descending below orange cliffs.

However, at the end of this short section the trail deteriorates into a rocky, boulder strewn, path which has suffered severe water erosion. For an alternative finish in **Taucho** see our Walk 14, 'Taucho Tour' route.

It's a long, tortuous, winding route down the mountainside requiring continuous concentration on what must be the roughest trail on the island - well cushioned footwear is absolutely essential. Having to concentrate on every footfall doesn't allow much opportunity to look at the scenery, and makes the last hour of the walk seem even longer. Eventually the downward toil finishes when we meet the tarmac (Wp.25) and stroll down the smooth surface to the start of the **Barranco del Infierno** walk (197M) at **Otello's** restaurant, though if it's Tuesday you'll need to continue down into **Adeje** for refreshment, and buses back to the resorts.

Here we have combined our easy route from **Vilaflor** to **La Escalona** with our original 'Walkers Who Lunch' to produce a delightful downhill stroll through bucolic countryside and rural settlements taking in the county town of **Arona** before finishing with a tarmac descent into **Valle San Lorenzo** where our choice is to lunch in **Café Paraiso** before bussing back to the resorts. All of country life is here and we make no apologies for much of the route being easy strolling on tarmac lanes; just the antidote to those hard mountain routes!

Access by bus: N°342 from **Playa de Las Américas** and **Los Cristianos**, N°482 from **Los Cristianos**. Return on the 416 or 418; the bus stop is just outside **Café Paraiso** in **Valle San Lorenzo**.

Access by car: linear route, not suited to car access.

We begin with a relaxed ride up to the first bus stop in **Vilaflor**, giving us a chance to look over the countryside that we'll be walking through. From the bus stop, we walk downhill to start out from **Snack Bar El Teide** (Wp.1 0M), from where we walk south, back down the TF-51 pavement to a dirt track heading right (Wp.2 4M W) beside the 'Bar Artesania' sign.

Climbing towards the crest before Wp.3

You can also reach this point by starting out along the TF-21 **Granadilla** road and then turn right to follow a village street which emerges onto the TF-51 at Wp.2.

Taking the dirt track, we face a steady ascent between old terraces to come up to the crest

The old waypost to Vilaflor

of a pine-dotted ridge by an old garage (Wp.3 13M).

Over the crest, we head downhill on the track past two small *embalses* before twisting down into the valley; as we cross the valley floor (Wp.4 22M) an old waypost marks a trail heading up the valley, an alternative route up to **Vilaflor**.

Directions are easy at this point as we stay on the track, gently descending the western side of the valley to come amongst Canarian pines before climbing over a small ridge to the solar-powered **Finca**

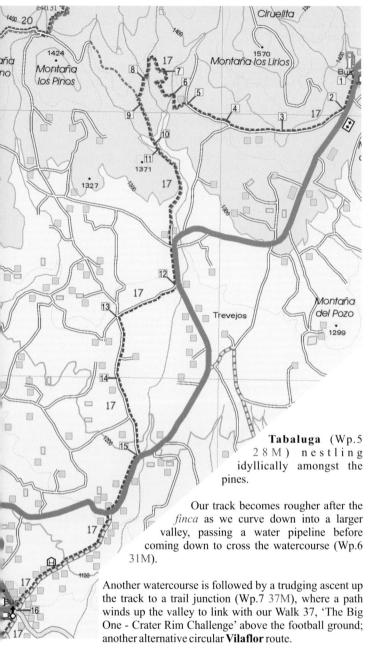

Tabaluga (Wp.5 28M) nestling idyllically amongst the pines.

Our track becomes rougher after the *finca* as we curve down into a larger valley, passing a water pipeline before coming down to cross the watercourse (Wp.6 31M).

Another watercourse is followed by a trudging ascent up the track to a trail junction (Wp.7 37M), where a path winds up the valley to link with our Walk 37, 'The Big One - Crater Rim Challenge' above the football ground; another alternative circular **Vilaflor** route.

Our track zigzags through the lower pine forest, becoming more water eroded as we progress, bringing us to a trio of cairns on the south of the track (Wp.8 44M); if you are using GPS, this junction is easy to spot, - it's important not to miss it.

The cleared area at the end of the *lomo*

Pine needles deeply cover the ground around the three cairns, hiding any sign of a path but as we head south amongst the trees and shrubs a cleared path appears; quite a well-walked path, as we pass an old rock wall on our right to run out onto a cleared area at the end of a *lomo* before coming amongst trees once again (Wp.9 48M).

The grey-rock waterfall

Now we steadily descend the line of a *lomo* between valleys, passing a cairn before clambering down to another cleared area.

Over a steel water pipe, we continue downhill on a hunters trail (Wp.10 53M) to join the trail coming down from the cairn; now we follow the line of a polished boulder watercourse, coming onto the boulders by a cairn (Wp.11 55M).

We head along the watercourse to the path's continuation on the right hand bank, above a dry grey-rock waterfall.

... above the developing gorge ..

Our narrow path crosses a large pipe which crosses the *barranco* on an aqueduct, as we continue above the developing gorge on our left, to views across to a staired descent accessing almond terraces in the *barranco* floor.

Ahead is the **Vilaflor** TF-51 road, as our trail widens out to a track running above the steep ravine before bringing us to the road.

We walk down the edge of the main road to a dirt road junction (Wp.12 74M) to go right on the main track (not the gated track), to head out into the farmlands of the **Ifonche** plateau. It's easy strolling, between low stone walls to reach a tarmac junction (Wp.13 81M) where we go left (S) signed for **Finca Trevejo**.

More easy strolling takes us past a *finca* (Wp.14 86M) with the unusual feature of a bird enclosure of almost aircraft hanger proportions, then on to a junction by **Finca Odette** where we keep straight ahead down between *embalses* for our track to run out onto the main road again by a 'Finca La Cucaracha' sign (Wp.15 95M).

At the sign for Finca Trevejo (Wp.13)

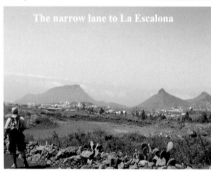
The narrow lane to La Escalona

Once more we walk down the main road, though you could take a track paralleling the TF-51 for part of the way, passing a horse riding centre before coming to the junction for **El Nogal**, a new upmarket country hotel that sits beside the narrow one-way lane dropping from the junction.

Taking the lane, an old donkey trail, then tarmacked and now thoughtfully restricted to one-way traffic, we have a steep descent accompanied by superb views.

At first there are only a few houses and the **Hotel El Nogal**, but after passing **Casa Blanca** (1925) our route becomes a terraced street dropping steeply down to the junctions opposite **La Escalona** square and church (Wp.16 110M), while ahead is the welcome sight of **Bar La Curva.**

La Escalona church square

After light refreshments we set off on the second part of our country adventure (0M) by narrow road that curves round from the bar, the **San Miguel** TF-565 road is on our the left, to the right past a small *ermita* to overlook the downhill continuation of our route.

Below us a vista of mountain slopes and peaks roll away to the coastal plain. The road, once the main donkey trail down to the county town of **Arona**, pays lip service to vehicles with a thin covering of tarmac, but few drivers know of or use this unmapped road. It is all downhill as the road drops steeply between farms, some working, others abandoned, and modern villas. Tarmac tracks lead off our narrow tarmac route, and terraces line both sides of the route,

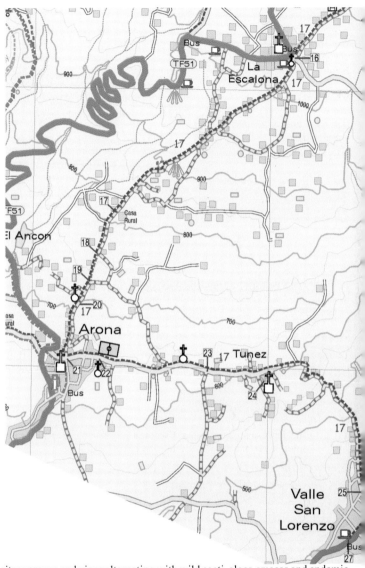

citrus groves and vines alternating with wild cacti, aloes, yuccas and endemic species.

Over on our right the mountains of **Conde** and **Imonde** dominate the landscape while we look down on the main road that climbs up the valley. Descending through this bucolic landscape, we pass old and new houses, this little route now becoming a popular place to build your large villa in the country, including the *Casa Rural* **Correa del Almendro** (Wp.17), until we come to where the *camino rural* swings sharp left (Wp.18).

Ahead, we go down a section of the old stone-laid donkey trail, passing an old farmhouse undergoing renovation, before rejoining the tarmac (Wp.19).

... a thoughtfully placed seat ...

A few metres on, we come to a cross and a thoughtfully placed bench seat (Wp.20) for a relaxed break at this point. The road continues steeply down, becomes **Calle San Antonio** and literally drops us down into the town square of **Arona** (Wp.21 38M).

At **Arona** there are bars off the town square for refreshment, and should you choose to finish walking here and return to the resort, continue straight over the town square down to the bus terminus from where the N°480 bus will take you to **Los Cristianos**.

We leave **Arona** on the **Túnez** road (turn left at the end of **Calle San Antonio**) past the **RACE** office. In contrast to our steep descent into **Arona,** the **Túnez** road undulates around the 600-metre contour, even going uphill to pass the football stadium on our left and a chapel on the right (Wp.22), before running along between a variety of homes ranging from simple habitations to Fort Knox style villas.

One view not to be missed, after we pass a *camino rural* off to our right (Wp.23), is an unusual garden on the right where modern sculptures and stonework mix with a Japanese style resulting in a most pleasing aspect. Passing the top of the property - note the hatchet and block - we find this most impressive of gardens is simply named N° 66. The next house, **La Esperanza**, was also briefly famous in the News of the World but is now better known for the large blue thing in its garden.

Strolling on, we pass **Túnez** church on our right (Wp.24) and head out into the country. Our road has narrowed, and when it swings right by a house and crosses a water canal, we start dropping down into the valley behind **Valle San Lorenzo**. Gentle strolling, with a few skittery steep sections, bring us down to the houses of the town and a Y-junction (Wp.25) where we go left.

Down the narrow street, we swing left and right to drop onto the main road (Wp.26) and go right. **Valle San Lorenzo** is in a state of parking gridlock - much easier to walk in and bus out - as we struggle past the petrol station (SW) to arrive at our destination (Wp.27 87M); **Caféteria Paraíso**.

Behind the simple exterior is one of the most popular eating places in the south of Tenerife with an extensive menu, good service and good prices (reservations essential in the evenings).

Also, the N°416/418 bus stop is just outside for the service down to **Los Cristianos**.

18 FANTASIA

When we pioneered this spectacular route on its (then) little known trails we never imagined that it would be made 'official'. But even the authorities know a good thing when they see it so the section from **Ifonche** to the edge of **Barranco del Rey** is now the **GR131**; see Walk 20. Whether it's mountains, spectacular views, a hidden valley, verdant plant life or unusual geology which you find most breathtaking, the sum of these parts is pure 'Fantasia' - truly one of the south's most spectacular walks.

Access by bus: We start by catching the N°342 or N°482 bus up to the **Ifonche** junction (**Cruce de Ifonche**) bus stop. From the junction we walk up the steep start of the **Ifonche** road to swing across the **Barranco de Funes** and climb up to the **Ifonche Plateau**. For the first hour we follow the quiet road down past **Bar Pedro** and past the turning to **El Refugio** (Wp.26), before dropping into the **Barranco de Ifonche** (Wp.28). Then it's a stiff climb up to **Bar El Dornajo** (Wp.29 3.2km), usually open from 13.00, in **Ifonche**. If you can get a lift or taxi to **Ifonche** you can reduce your walking time by an hour.

At **El Dornajo** we turn left (S) to walk along the narrow road, passing another tiny road going up to the left while we continue straight on. As we stroll down below a terrace wall, away on our right is an impressive farming settlement, its massive terrace walls giving the look of a fortified promontory. After running downhill the road climbs quite steeply up to a house before levelling out to run along a ridge, then we come to a road junction with a sturdy wooden cross set in a concrete base (Wp.1 4km) where a road drops down into the valley on our left.

Access by car: Follow the same directions as for bus travellers and park near the wooden cross; parking at **El Dornajo** is often rather fraught.

From the cross (Wp.1 0M) we stroll along the ridge on the lane heading towards **Roque Imonde**. On our right we pass the head-shaped rock outcrop of Garcia's Nose to come under the heights of **Roque de los Brezos**. Our lane descends gently through Canarian pines as we walk above abandoned terraces on our left, undulating along below **Roque de los Brezos** to come above cultivated terraces and a farm house. Ahead is the saddle between the *roques* of **Imonde** and **los Brezos** which is our first destination; now marked by a GR131 waypoint..

As the road swings left to run down to the farmhouse, look for a path (Wp.2 8M) which runs below the ridge to cross the open ground and climb gently up to the saddle. If you miss the first path, look for the official GR131 trail further down towards the farmhouse. N.B. Do not go past the farmhouse on the lane as its backyard is filled with hunting dogs and a couple of guard dogs!

As we reach the saddle, a spectacular view over **Playa de las Américas** welcomes our arrival. Set on the saddle is a large *era* (Wp.3) dating from the old days when the terraced slopes of **Roque Imonde** were cultivated.

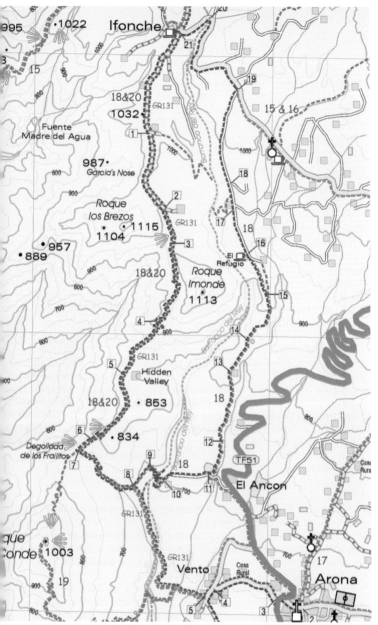

Before it became the GR131 the trail off the saddle was difficult to spot but now we simply walk over to the waypost to take the 'upgraded' trail running down the west side of the mountain. What was a narrow path is now a trenched stone-littered trail making for a picky descent before a small ascent brings us up onto the top of the spur to overlook the gentle landscape of the 'hidden valley' (Wp.4). Neat though abandoned terraces ring this bowl in the mountains, where in spring field marigolds create a golden carpet, adding to the atmosphere.

Roque Imonde

Our GR131 trail runs down the promontory passing below an *era* (Wp.5 40M), set on the saddle between the rounded hills after which a steep rock descent drops us down to pass an area of shattered rock (Wp.6 52M) after which our route is easier as it takes us onto a trail junction on the **Degollada de los Frailitos** saddle between **Imonde** and **Conde** (Wp.7).

Views over Adeje

Straight ahead a trail leads to the northern ascent/descent of **Roque del Conde** while the **GR131** turns left (SE) to head down a shallow valley.

From the *degollada* we used to have a picky descent down to the valley floor which is now replaced by the GR131 manicured trail making for an easy drop down to the watercourse running along the valley floor. Here the GR131 trail simply follows the northern side of the watercourse, where our original path crossed and re-crossed the dry watercourse, with the great bulk of **Roque del Conde** looming over us on our right as we have an easy stroll down to a trail junction (Wp.8) marked by a GR131 waypost. Here the GR131 heads south to meet the **Roque del Conde** trail before crossing the *barrancos* into **Vento** - see Walks 19 & 20.

Where the GR131 goes right ,we continue straight ahead on the (now) minor trail which brings us to the lip of the **Barranco del Rey** and along to the top of an old *sendero* donkey trail dropping into the *barranco* (Wp.9 70M). It's a steep, zigzagging descent requiring careful footwork before we emerge on the floor of the *barranco* by a 'pa' sign; just the place to take a cool break in the shade (mornings) before tackling the long ascent back to **Ifonche**.

A few metres down the *barranco* we come to the restart of the *sendero*. It is onwards and upwards on the boulder-laid trail to steadily climb up through a series of zigzags, taking rests when necessary. The path levels out at an area of red earth below small cliffs, giving us *mirador* views back over a landscape untouched by man for decades. From the red earth, the path runs along the lip of the *barranco* below the cliffs before turning left to climb up over rock and away from the ravine on a rough path to come alongside abandoned terraces.

The tiled roof of a cottage comes into view as our route follows the edge of the terraces to pass behind the cottage (Wp.10), from where we follow a rough donkey trail up between tumbled stone walls, passing a disused water cistern on our right, to come onto a dirt road. It's a gentle stroll along the dirt road as it starts to run downhill to come below the wall of an *embalse* (Wp.11 86M).

We now start to pay for all that downhill as we go up a rocked-off dirt road signed to **El Refugio**. Coming up round the *embalse*, we face slopes of abandoned farm land stretching up to the horizon. A rough path, well waymarked with white splodges, takes us up between the picturesque **Barranco del Ancon** and a large water channel. It is a steady, relentless ascent which can distract from the beautiful views, to cross a metal water pipe before coming up to a tumbled cottage (Wp.12 108M). After the cottage the gradient eases for us to stroll up to a circular water tank (Wp.13) and cross the water channel to walk across to abandoned terraces.

Now the ascent starts again as the white splodged path takes us up through the old terraces onto a steep section of the path which brings a white house into view. Before reaching the house white splodges guide us off the path (Wp.14) to climb up onto a really rough old rock road. A stiff climb takes us past the white house and onto a dirt road with the welcoming sight of **El Refugio** ahead; a final few metres bring us up to this unique hostelry (Wp.15 133M).

From **El Refugio** we head up the dirt road to pass a goat farm on our left and dirt road to the right (Wp.16). For the adventurous we can short cut back to our start point by descending into **Barranco del Rey** on a donkey trail behind the goat farm, though unfortunately the continuation on the far slope has been long abandoned leading to a lively ascent - see map for paths which are linked by walking along the polished boulder watercourse. Our choice is to continue up the dirt road to the **Ifonche** road (Wp.17 149M) to turn left and follow the tarmac. We drop down into the **Barranco del Rey** the road swinging left across its watercourse (Wp.18 159M) where a **Vilaflor** walking route is signed off the road. A steep climb brings us up to **El Dornajo** (Wp.19) for the possibility of more refreshment before heading out on the narrow tarmac lane to our starting point (Wp.1 174M).

Roque del Conde's 1000 metre 'table top' peak dominates the coastal plain of southern Tenerife. The views from the top are simply stupendous, rewarding the stiff climb up this impressive mountain, which also appeals to plant enthusiasts. This route is for fit walkers who can confidently tackle a climb totalling 450 metres on rough tracks requiring good, well cushioned, walking footwear.

Access by car: Our starting point is at the junction of the **Vento** road with the TF-51, just above **Arona**'s town square, where there's plenty of parking; please do not park on the narrow roads in **Vento** village.

Access by bus: Bus N°s 480 and 482 take you from **Playa de las Américas/Los Cristianos** to the **Arona** terminus. Walk up the street to the town square to take the **Calle Prolongacion D'Alfonso** from the north-west corner of the square. Climbing up the steep street, we then cross carefully over the main road to start point by the **GR131** waypost.

From the GR131 waypost (Wp.1 0M), we climb up from the main road to views down to the coast as the lane swings left and past **La Casa del Pintur** *casa rural* (Wp.**2**) before the lane runs down between the first houses of **Vento**.

We stroll down to the religious obelisk at the T-junction (Wp.3 6M) and turning left we come down to the **Roque del Conde/GR131** path (Wp.4) which is signed off to our right by house N°78. A wall plaque over a green painted shutter immediately after we've turned right informs us that this house was built in 1852.

On the well-made *sendero*

The 1852 wall plaque

After the tarmac we are on a well-made *sendero* which drops us down into the **Barranco de las Casas** (Wp.5). Our trail runs up over rock to a crest and then drops us down the **Barranco del Ancón** (Wp.6). Across the valley floor, a gentle climb brings us up alongside the

barranco, passing a path off to our left (Wp.7), until our trail swings right across a water channel to a junction of paths. We go straight ahead over rock to a 'pa' sign (Wp.8) and confront the **Barranco del Rey**.

At the lip of the *barranco* wall we come onto a well-made *sendero* which zigzags steeply down towards the *barranco* floor. Stone walls with posts mounted in them line the *sendero*, as we drop down on its rough boulder surface.

After twists and turns we come onto the valley floor (Wp.9 22M) just above a waterfall (after rainfall) with sheer cliff walls rising fifty metres up on each side of us.

Straight across the valley floor, we come onto another rough boulder *sendero* marked by white arrows, and start climbing. We toil up the stiff climb, which gets steeper as we get higher, until a set of stone steps brings up to the top of the *barranco* wall (Wp.10). Ahead, **Roque del Conde** looms over us as the **GR131** trail goes right while we take the path to the left. Climbing up past a white arrow, our dirt path winds it way up to a gold rock slab, with views back to **Vento**, and continues on towards a crumbling cottage.

Over a small crest the path runs down past a small water cistern the size of a bath, on our right (Wp.11). Above the water cistern, unseen by most walkers, is an opening in the rock. Climbing up the rock slope, we find ourselves looking through the narrow opening into a large subterranean cavern. A small channel, now mostly silted up, guides water into the cavern. In the far distant past, long before pipes and water channels, this substantial cistern was the main water storage in this area. You can get an idea of the cavern's size by shouting into it and waiting for the echo! Leaving this historical site we drop back down onto the path to continue on to the cottage (Wp.12 30M).

Our trail climbs up past the north wall of the cottage. We pass two threshing circles on our left (Wps.13 & 14) as we continue up over the abandoned terraces to come onto a boulder-laid donkey trail (Wp.15) to continue straight uphill. Our trail swings left for us to head diagonally across the slope in a

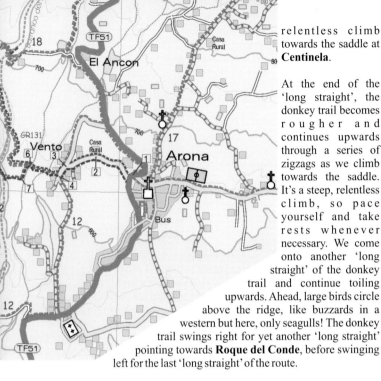

relentless climb towards the saddle at **Centinela**.

At the end of the 'long straight', the donkey trail becomes rougher and continues upwards through a series of zigzags as we climb towards the saddle. It's a steep, relentless climb, so pace yourself and take rests whenever necessary. We come onto another 'long straight' of the donkey trail and continue toiling upwards. Ahead, large birds circle above the ridge, like buzzards in a western but here, only seagulls! The donkey trail swings right for yet another 'long straight' pointing towards **Roque del Conde**, before swinging left for the last 'long straight' of the route.

At the end of the last 'long straight' we swing right and the donkey trail finishes for us to continue climbing on a narrow dirt path. We climb steeply up through a series of zigzags to reach the saddle at **Centinela** (Wp.16 51M). The path opens out into a small clear area, forming an unofficial *mirador*. As we climb onto the ridge, spectacular views open up over the resort of **Playa de las Américas** over 700 metres below us.

We take a break on the *mirador* to enjoy the vistas laid out below us. Our start point in **Arona** can be seen 150 metres below our present position to the east; this difference in altitude leads us to question our next step.

From the *mirador* it is a narrow, often rough, path which includes steep climbs totalling 250 metres to the top of **Roque del Conde**, and 250 metres back down (of course) to the *mirador*. If at this point you are very tired, then rest here before returning the same way down to **Vento** and **Arona**. Similarly, if you encounter bad weather, or if **Conde** has become cloud covered, finish at **Centinela** and return to **Arona**.

From **Centinela** a narrow path goes right (NW) along the ridge towards **Roque del Conde**, marked by white paint. Our route undulates along to take us across the southern face of the mountain until we swing right (Wp.17) for a zigzag ascent. We come above the hidden valley which lies behind **Playa de las Américas**, the head of the valley and one ridge filled with *embalses* while the floor is covered with banana plantations. The loose rock and dirt path climbs steeply to bring us up onto sheets of orange rock below ten metre high cliffs (Wp.18).

Going left, we continue to circle the mountain following the trail as it climbs around rock promontories. It is onwards and upwards through a series of steep climbs, the path splitting (Wp.19) and rejoining (Wp.20) just above a 'TS4' white paint marker.

Breathtaking views north from the peak

A final toiling ascent brings us onto the edge of the plateau (Wp.21 83M), and a surprise. On the mountain-top we find long abandoned agricultural terraces - sometime in the distant past someone used to farm this least accessible area of land!

Asphodels on the plateau

A path, trodden down by walkers, leads across the terraces towards the mound and height marker at the official peak of **Roque del Conde**. As we approach the peak we find the large mound covered in a sea of asphodels (Asphodelus tenuifolius), a beautiful sight when in flower from February to May. Pushing through the flowers we come to the height marker (Wp.22 88M).

Roque del Conde is the final mountain in the chain surrounding **Las Cañadas**, and inland is the 'turret' peak of **Roque Imonde**.

Awesome views south

From here, standing suspended high above the surrounding lands, we have awesome views over the south and west coasts - a fitting reward for our efforts.

We return by the same route taking care on the steep descent down to the *mirador*, after which the path and donkey trail make for an easier descent, though it can be hard on the knees. The climbs out of the three *barrancos*, particularly **Barranco del Rey**, give us a reminder of our earlier efforts before we arrive back at **Arona**. There is an 'experts only' route down the north face of Conde which joins Walks 18 & 20 at the **Degollada de los Frailitos** for the adventurous seeking a circular route taking in **Roque del Conde**.

Tenerife's new **GR131** long distance walking route is a welcome official addition to the island's extensive network of hiking routes. We already cover parts of the it in walks 5, 18, 35, 36, 37 and 39, so we've selected the largely new final section from **Vilaflor** to **Arona** via **Ifonche** as the newly created trails have opened up previously inaccessible areas to walkers; plus it's a route with a top class *tipico* restaurant (**El Dornajo**) at approximately the half way point.

While this route has a number of signs and wayposts, it still pays to read and follow the detailed walk description as a couple of important junctions are not signed, such as waypoint 15. For the first half of the route we're in the pine forests, following a series of old trails that have been linked together to form part of the **GR131**, before descending to **Ifonche**. We then follow our Fantasia route, enjoying exceptional views until taking the newly-made **GR131** trail at waypoint 27, to link with our Table Mountain route for our finish in **Arona**.

On the descent towards **Ifonche** there is a small vertigo risk on some sections of the 'Striding Edge' descent, though the worst sections have sturdy wooden safety fences installed. Combining such a range of scenery, views, and refreshments this route is destined to become a modern classic of Tenerife.

Access by bus: Nº342 or 482 to **Vilaflor**. Nº480 or 482 for return from **Arona**.

Access by car: Ideally you should arrange a two car expedition, leaving one car in **Arona** and then driving the other car up to the parking area by the hotel and sports ground at waypoint 4. At the end of the route you simply drive the first car up to pick up your second car. This is the most efficient arrangement plus you cut out the first 1.3 kilometres of road walking with its 100+ metre ascent, quite the most boring and laborious section of the whole route.
If you are a one car group then we suggest parking in **Arona** and catching the Nº482 bus for the ride up to **Vilaflor**.

Extension to the Walking Route
If you are looking for a longer hike in the southern mountains then you could take the Nº342 bus up to the **Las Lajas** recreation area to follow the second part of Walk 38 descending to meet the **GR131** at waypoint 6. Add two and a quarter hours to the hiking time.

Bus start walking route
Arriving by bus, you'll be dropped off at the bottom of **Vilaflor** village by the petrol station (Wp.1 0M) from where we face a steady uphill slog along the main road passing a number of bar/cafes before coming to the first street on our left (Wp.2). We could go up this street, but as it's extremely steep, our preferred route (walking or driving) is to continue up the main road to the second street (Wp.3) where we face a steep enough ascent before the gradient

relents to steady for us to continue up to the hotel where we find the first **GR131** signpost 'Ifonche 10.2km Arona 16.7km' at the end of the parking area (Wp.4 30M), our start point for 'two car' groups.

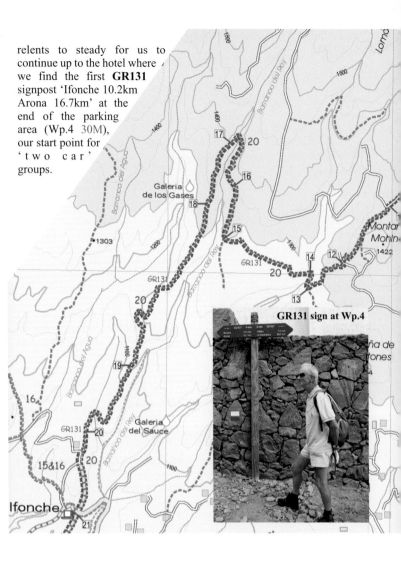

GR131 sign at Wp.4

'Two Car' start for the main walking route

Leaving the parking area (0M) we go steadily uphill on the dirt track passing a track off to our right and vegetable plots before a steeper climb brings us up to a junction of tracks (Wp.5) where we go right following a 'Las Lajas' sign nailed to a tree. It's a steep climb up the rough track bringing us to a roofed *embalse* before a steady

The sign nailed to a tree near Wp.5

LAS LAJAS

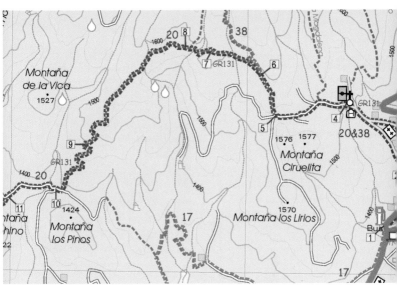

ascent up to a GR131 waypost (Wp.6 12M, 'Ifonche 9.2km').

Taking the new **GR131** trail, we head west through pine-covered slopes to a junction marked with a cairn (Wp.7 21M). We continue ahead on the main 'manicured' trail to cross a *barranco*.

Then it's down into another ravine, followed by another climb onto the *lomo* (Wp.8) between *barrancos* with a stone-built table and *mirador* views down over the southern vistas. Although our route is generally downhill all the way, it is punctuated by these *barranco* crossings until we've crossed the largest, **Barranco del Rey**, directly above **Ifonche**.

Passing another stone table amongst the pines, we continue down and up through another *barranco* before our descent stays on a *lomo*, bringing us down through a waymarked hairpin bend (Wp.9). Continuing down to a water change point below, we come onto a dirt track (Wp.10 65M) marked with a **GR131** waypost and a 'trail restrictions' sign.

Short Walk Option
The trail runs east to cultivated terraces and according to the map, runs out into a trail which links with Walk 17, giving the option of a circular return route to **Vilaflor**.

We are now amongst the dirt tracks above the **Ifonche** plateau often used by quad bikers, so watch out for traffic amongst these forested slopes! Going west, we pass a waypost 'Ifonche 6.7km' at a track junction shortly before coming to a clearing around a large pine, almost like a roundabout amongst the forest, where the dirt track heads down into a *barranco*.

We take the **GR131** signed trail, leaving the dirt track behind (Wp.11 73M) to head steadily downhill through the trees. We pass a red and white waymark before our trail crosses a minor dirt track (Wp.12), coming from an abandoned cottage. Coming down the *lomo*, we arrive at its nose to overlook cultivated areas before heading down into the next ravine.

The Guajero stone bridge at Wp.14

Two waypoints keep us on the trail where a water runoff could be confused for a walking route, before we descend to a junction (Wp.13) with a trail joining us from the left. Now it's down into the *barranco* where a safety fence protects us from a vertiginous section before we drop down (literally) to the picturesque **Guajero** stone bridge (Wp.14). The sheer-sided *barranco* along with the stone bridge presents some of the most dramatic scenery on this section of the **GR131** so we take a few minutes enjoying this dramatic landscape before continuing on the well-made trail.

Climbing up out of the *barranco*, we cross a area of rock to head for a water channel with a cairn alongside a potato field above a modern house. Across the water channel, we continue up (WNW) across another rock sheet guided by red and white waymarks to come up to a water change point above a small reservoir. Previously we had been heading west and south-west downhill towards **Ifonche** but now we're heading west north-west in a steady climb away from **Ifonche** - it's tempting to be looking for a trail going left (south) but after dipping into and climbing out of a small *barranco* we come to a junction (Wp.15) where a trail does indeed head south - this is one junction that really should have a **GR131** sign as the correct trail is north uphill.

Now our trail heads up the eastern side of **Barranco del Rey** in a steady climb where a red and white waymark (Wp.16) confirms we're on the correct route. We continue climbing until the trail dips down to cross the water course before climbing up the western side to the peak of the path (Wp.17 140M).

Reassuring news at Wp.20

Now we have a comfortable downhill stroll as we head down the *lomo* between two *barrancos* (S) to pass an era (Wp.18 149M) as the *lomo* narrows to a 'striding edge' descent, the ravine's walls dropping sheer beside the path. We need to pick our way carefully down the trail as fallen pine needles can make for slippery surfaces on the rock, and always stop if you want to look at this spectacular landscape. Wooden safety fences (Wp.19) protect us from a vertiginous section before we drop down into a *barranco* before climbing steeply up to a waypost (Wp.20) telling us the reassuring news that **Ifonche** is just 0.6kms ahead.

We come onto a dirt track for an easy downhill stroll, the track becoming tarmacked before it finally drops us down to the crossroads outside **El Dornajo** (closed Mondays) (Wp.21 190M). To come across a well-recommended restaurant in the middle of wild countryside is an unusual event, so we take full advantage by stopping for lunch. Pork and rabbit are the specialties but not much for vegetarians.

Second part of the main walking route

From **El Dornajo**, following an enjoyable lunch (so timings might be a tad slower than normal) we follow the route pioneered in our Fantasia walk for over three kilometres, the official **GR131** having made this previously little known trail into the equivalent of a walking motorway.

From the crossroads outside the restaurant (Wp.21 0M), we head south along a tarmac lane for an easy stroll, keeping to the main lane when branches go off to our left, the second at a cross - the start point for Fantasia - to pass below a paraglider launch point (Wp.22 13M) at **Garcia's Nose**. As **Roque Los Brezos** rises on our right, our lane starts to run downhill to its end at a farm with noisy dogs.

Here we are looking for a faint trail (Wp.23 15M) leaving the lane by a white-topped marker; the official path leaves the lane a hundred metres further down the lane but offers no better route out to the saddle between **Brezos** and **Imonde**. A myriad of faint paths, including the official one, lead across the broken ground to bring us over to the **GR131** signboard alongside the *era* on the saddle (Wp.24) giving us one of the most spectacular views in the south.

Our **GR131**/Fantasia trail starts with a wooden safety fence as it heads down below the slopes of **Imonde** (S then SW) with a steep *barranco* developing on our right. The trail has been 'improved' by being slightly channelled to avoid a slip to the right, but the result is that with more walkers and water runoff, the channel has become littered with shale sized rocks making for a very picky descent; views are spectacular but always 'stop to look at the view'. Underfoot conditions improve as we approach the *era* above the abandoned farm in **Hidden Valley** (Wp.25 48M) for us to continue down on rock, stepped in places. Our trail drops below the ridge line, cutting out the view, before emerging to *mirador* views and then dropping down to a junction on the **Degollada de los Frailitos** (Wp.26 64M).

Ahead is a new path to the northern descent from **Roque del Conde** while we follow the main trail left (SE) as it descends into a shallow valley beneath the lower slopes of **Roque del Conde**. After the earlier picky descent this is a relaxed downhill stroll following our Fantasia route until we meet a **GR131** waypost (Wp.27 76M) where 'Fantasia' continues ahead while we turn right on the new **GR131** trail which heads along the *lomo* (SE) between two *barrancos*.

We pass an *era* threshing circle on our left just before the ruins of cottages alongside our solid rock trail after which our trail descends to a new crossing of the **Barranco del Rey**. Just above the ravine floor is a cairn seat, if you fancy a rest before climbing up onto another rock *lomo*. Our clear trail curves above the **Barranco del Rey**, protected by a wooden safety fence before it runs on to meet the **Roque del Conde** trail above the final ravine crossing (Wp.29).

Another descent to the *barranco* floor is followed by a steep ascent up the well-made trail to bring us onto the end of a small, steep street (Wp.30). From here we climb up to join the main street of **Vento**, turn left and then right at the memorial for a final stroll along the quiet lane, passing a *casa rural* before coming down to the main road parking area above **Arona**'s town square (Wp.32) with the final **GR131** signpost showing 'Ifonche 6.2km'.

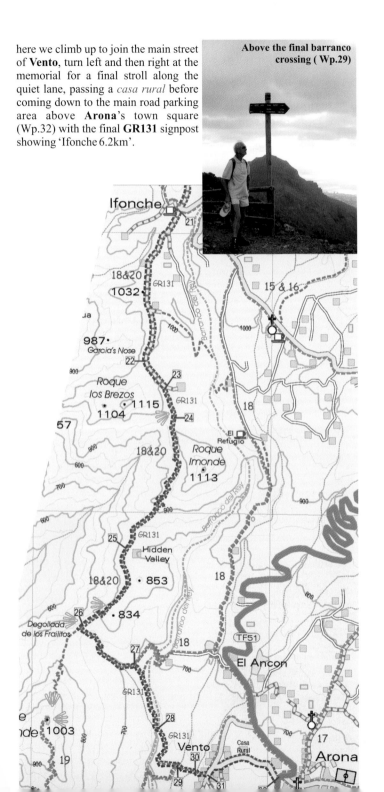

Above the final barranco crossing (Wp.29)

Ifonche
21

18&20
1032
GR131

15 & 16

1000

1000

Ja

987
García's Nose
22

900

Roque
los Brezos
1104 • 1115
57

23

GR131

24

18

El
Refugio

18&20

Roque
Imonde
1113

Barranco del Rey

800

700

900

600

900

GR131
25

Hidden
Valley

18&20 • 853

18

600

26 • 834

Degollada
de los Frailitos

27

18

TF51

El Ancon

GR131

28

GR131

Vento
30

Casa
Rural

17

Arona

nde 1003

19

29

31

Little-used paths (by walkers) take us down the western edge of the valley below **Santiago del Teide** through a mixture of bucolic countryside before coming onto a spectacular ridge for *mirador* views over the wild west of Tenerife, then descending on an old donkey trail to **Tamaimo**. Exceptional examples of endemic flora pack our route which soon leaves civilisation, though the distant sound of traffic is always with us.

This relatively leisurely linear walk can be made circular by using the final section of Walk 23, 'True Grit' up to **El Retamar**; then either 'True Grit' across the *malpaís* and its alternative finish to **Santiago del Teide**, or take the *camino rural* from **El Retamar** (our choice) up to **El Molledo** to join our outward route.

3   2H   7 km   130m / 470m   2*

* in **Tamaimo**

Access by bus: Service N°s 460 links **Playa de las Américas** and **Icod de Los Vinos** via **Santiago del Teide** and **Tamaimo**, a fascinating bus adventure in its own right. From **Puerto de la Cruz**, take the N°325or there's the N°462 between **Los Gigantes** and **Guía de Isora**.

Access by car: There is usually on-street parking on the main street of **Santiago del Teide**, or carry on past the church to park alongside the shady picnic area on the left on the northern edge of the village.

Our start point is the centre of **Santiago del Teide** by the **Masca** junction, opposite the church, (Wp.1 0M). Strolling south along the pavement, we come to the ornate arch and bridge (Wp.2 5M) for the **Fuente de la Virgen**. The bridge takes us over a water course, then under a second arch we come onto the **Camino de la Virgen de Lourdes**. A dirt trail takes us across the meadow before we start to climb an out-flung spur of **Montaña Ijada**, where the route becomes a stone-laid donkey trail.

The route is 'waymarked' by fourteen two metre high crosses, each with a plaque depicting a stage of the **Calvario**. Past the first cross, there's an energetic climb as we follow the signed route after the third cross (Wp.3) rather than taking the short cut to the sixth cross. At a spoil heap a dirt path goes straight ahead (Wp.4) while we continue ascending on the stone-laid trail.

The steady climb finally brings us to the fourteenth cross where the trail swings right to climb diagonally across the slope to a *mirador* at a hairpin bend overlooking the village. After taking in the views we ascend through the bend to make a last

Santiago del Teide, from the *ermita*

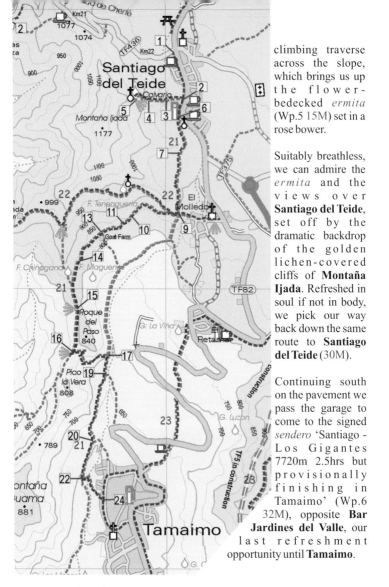

climbing traverse across the slope, which brings us up the flower-bedecked *ermita* (Wp.5 15M) set in a rose bower.

Suitably breathless, we can admire the *ermita* and the views over **Santiago del Teide**, set off by the dramatic backdrop of the golden lichen-covered cliffs of **Montaña Ijada**. Refreshed in soul if not in body, we pick our way back down the same route to **Santiago del Teide** (30M).

Continuing south on the pavement we pass the garage to come to the signed *sendero* 'Santiago - Los Gigantes 7720m 2.5hrs but provisionally finishing in Tamaimo' (Wp.6 32M), opposite **Bar Jardines del Valle**, our last refreshment opportunity until **Tamaimo**.

We step out along the broad grassy trail (S) with the slopes of **Montaña Ijada** away on our right, easy walking through this bucolic landscape of stone-walled fields only occasionally in cultivation. The main road has swung away east as we pass a copse of stately palms on our left and a collapsed terrace wall (Wp.7) and here the gentle nature of the route starts to change as the trail narrows and drops down between high boulder walls on a lumpy stone-laid base, before continuing as a dirt path which runs alongside abandoned fields.

Our trail is increasingly stone-littered as we descend gently towards **El Molledo**, looking over the village as our path runs across a large slab of rock at the end of a spur.

The views then open up down to the ocean, the path becoming rough as it descends above cultivated plots to meet the wide stone-laid donkey trail of Walk 22, 'An OK Corral' (Wp.8 42M). Down below us is the second way marking sign for the continuation of the 'official' *sendero*, and an alternative return route for a circular walk, as we turn right to climb up (W) over rock to a path junction (Wp.9 44M) where 'OK Corral' takes the right fork while we go down to the left.

The rock and dirt trail with occasional stone-laid sections takes us steadily down the valley wall (W), great swathes of coloured rock and vertically grained rock 'fences' running down from the steep slopes above us. A steel water pipe runs alongside our route as we turn round a spur (Wp.10 51M) to see our trail running ahead around the valley wall. It is downhill on the rough path, crossing a boulder-choked gully (Wp.11) before undulating along to the corrals (Wp.12) and buildings (Wp.13 57M) of an abandoned goat farm.

The farm's large flock of goats are cute, but they've churned up our path beyond the farm, so careful footwork is needed as we climb over a spur and into a pocket in the valley wall, before our route climbs higher above the valley floor to an outcrop of red rock making a natural *mirador* (Wp.14). From the outcrop we pass **Fuente Chiñagana** leaking water into two small pools, suitable only for animal consumption. Beyond the *fuente* we continue on the gritty, goat-churned path (S), dropping then climbing up to a saddle on the ridge (Wp.15 67M).

... impressive western panorama ...

Once on the ridge before **Roque del Paso** we are treated to an impressive western panorama, including **Roque Blanco** and **Barranco de la Mancha de los Diaz** - camera essential.

From the saddle, our route drops steeply down the western side of **Roque del Paso** on a boulder-laid trail.

Our trail becomes littered by rock flakes which have shattered from the rock face on our left before taking on an alternately flat then up-and-down nature to reach a junction on another saddle (Wp.16 77M), south of the peak. The views in this area are all five-star.

A Diversion
Our onward route goes east (E) at this point, though the energetic can take a demanding diversion into the **Barranco Mancha de los Diaz**. Continuing on the southerly trail, we zigzag steeply into the *barranco* on a deteriorating trail down the ravine's sheer wall, our concentration rewarded as we reach a 'lawned' promontory, suspended beneath the mountain and the *barranco*, surrounded by superb views. It is a picnic spot with few equals.

Near the edge of Barranco Seco

Although the trail continues down **Barranco Seco** to the sea, then climbs 800 metres to **Morro de la Vera**, it is a deteriorating trail with high vertigo risk that requires high levels of endurance, so we recommend only our short diversion to the 'lawn'.

We return by the same route to the saddle.

Continuation

From the saddle we take a little-used path (NE) which runs below the eroded southern face of **Morro de la Vera**.

This path was made for the tunnel workers; there's a water canal runs from **Tamaimo** to **Barranco de la Mancha de los Diaz**.

Goats keep much of the western section open, but our route has suffered from erosion and is becoming overgrown; secateurs are very useful. Concentration is necessary on the overgrown loose boulder trail, as we head downhill to a hairpin bend, secateurs again useful as we progress along traverses and through hairpin bends. After hairpin Nº9 we come below a large cave, the peak now hidden from view, and after hairpin Nº13 we encounter a large fallen rock, followed by a fallen terrace wall a little further on. Picking our way over the stones, we come back onto the path which winds down the slope to join the route of the 'official' *sendero* (Wp.17 89M).

For a circular route

- turn left (N) and follow the trail back up to **El Molledo**.

Turning right (S) we follow the narrow trail downhill alongside a steel water pipe; the pipe swinging left across the watercourse (Wp.18) just before a faint walking trail (Wp.19) that follows the pipe. It's a steady trudge down the path to pass a large pine (Wp.20 100M) and abandoned terraces above our route (Wp.21) before coming down to a junction (Wp.22 106M) where a little used stone-laid trail climbs to our front right.

Here we turn left to skitter down a rock-laid slope, then cross the water course onto slabs of rock. Curving south, we continue on rock slabs until we spot a glass-littered dirt path (Wp.23) which takes us up to the first houses of **Tamaimo** (Wp.24) and onto a tarmac street.

At the end of the tiny street is a T-junction; left is steeply uphill and then right to climb up to the top of the town, but easier by far is to go right and then work our way through the old town to the main road (117M), refreshments and bus services.

If you're looking for a simple, safe route into the spectacular *barrancos* of the west coast, this walk is for you. With easy bus or car access, well-made trails and stunning views, this route has everything except a refreshment *tipico*.

Access by car: Car drivers should turn off the main TF-82 road into **El Molledo** at the bus stop and park by the village square and church.

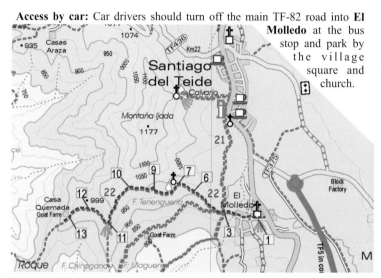

Access by bus: Our start is at the TF-82 bus stop for **El Molledo**. From **Playa de las Américas** use bus N° 460; from **Puerto de la Cruz**, take the N°325, from **Los Gigantes** the N°462 between **Los Gigantes** and **Guía de Isora**.
From the bus stop we follow **Calle La Tagora** to the village square and church (Wp.1 0M). Coming to a cross roads, we continue straight over (W) onto **Calle Calzada** and drop steeply downhill until we face house N°16. Here we turn right on a track between white walls and boulder walls to cross a water run-off (Wp.2) and come onto a stone-laid donkey trail.

Our trail climbs up to a junction (Wp.3) where the route down to **Tamaimo** is signed left, while we continue to climb steadily to another junction (Wp.4) where the path from **Santiago del Teide** comes down the hillside to join us. Keeping to the main path, we come to a third junction (Wp.5 5M) where a path runs down the wall of the valley (Walk 21, 'Wild West Tour'), while our route is the higher path to the right.

We start the steady, continuous climb up around the edge of a bowl in the valley wall, the lower path running parallel but soon far below us. Excellent views (stop to look) compensate for the energetic ascent on a mixture of stone-laid trail and rock slopes in reds and yellows (Wp.6).

Across the bowl we notice another pair of waymarking posts, then the gradient eases as we approach a corner in the bowl, just past which a Madonna statue and cross occupy a cave just above the path (Wp.7). Our trail continues as a comfortable dirt path which leads to the waymarking posts, which are missing their signboard, and the **Fuente Tenengueria** built in 1936 (Wp.8 14M) with a working water tap.

The path is easy to follow as we leave the posts and *fuente* behind and resume our ascent of the plant-covered slope as the track swings west, flattens out and then climbs again, our narrow path wriggling up towards the ridge line above. In this barely accessible, seemingly uncultivateable land, a stiff climb brings us up to two tiny walled terraces set in a small pocket in the valley wall (Wp.9), our route zigzagging steeply past them. In places the route is not clearly defined as it crosses sheets of rock, but a low stone wall keeps us on track to reach a purple rock *mirador*, just the place to take a break and enjoy the panoramic views across to **La Hoya**.

Notice the natural rock arch in the ridge above us as we set off again, on a gentle ascent up to a precariously balanced large boulder (Wp.10). Scuttling beneath the boulder, we descend into a pocket in the valley wall where our trail turns left above a large cleft. Grasses push in on the narrow path as we stroll (S) between the ridge and the long drop to the valley floor, the ridge gradually becoming less prominent as it comes down to meet our path (Wp.11 31M). Now new vistas open up across **Barranco Mancha de los Diaz**, and following the line of the ridge we zigzag down onto a saddle - the views are impressive!

At Casa Quemada goat farm

From the saddle we go down the knobbly rock sheets, following the line of a low boulder wall to reach a trail which we take down into the head of the *barranco*, a steep, almost staired descent which then levels out to follow a contour line around the bowl in the head of the *barranco*.

We curve around towards abandoned terraces, **Casa Quemada** goat farm hidden from view for now. A climb up through the terraces takes us towards an overhanging rock outcrop, from where (Wp.12 43M) we enjoy stupendous views along the length of the west. A cairn of white-splashed rocks mark the path's continuation off the outcrop, leading us onto a clearly defined trail which heads towards the goat farm with its fences, gates and noisy guard dogs (chained). The couple who run this isolated agricultural enterprise 'commute' from **El Molledo**, carrying the goat feed with them!

An old threshing circle (Wp.13 47M) alongside the corral makes an 'OK' *mirador*, but continuing onto the spur which runs down from the corral to **Roque Blanco** reveals dramatic views into **Barranco del Natero**, while if you look inland you'll see tourist hire cars lined up on the distant **Masca** road. We return by the same route.

Some walks have it all; varied landscapes, spectacular views, masses of endemic flora, great geology and refreshments. This is such a walk with the added advantage of *tipicos* located just where you need them! Surprisingly, no other walkers appear to know of this route so you won't be bothered by multi-coloured paint splashes spoiling the natural beauty. Definitely a 'Western Classic'.

Sadly the new TF-5 road works have impinged on our classic western tour meaning we've lost the classic donkey trail into **Arguayo**, now replaced by road walking, plus crossing a new pedestrian bridge (or the incomplete roadway) in the **Tamaimo** valley. **Bar El Cercado** is closed and for sale, our **Arguayo** refreshments now catered for by **Bar Tropic**. Despite these changes, True Grit remains a true 'Western Classic'.

Access by bus: Bus Nº460 from **Playa de las Américas**, and Nºs 462 & 325 from **Los Gigantes** serve **Tamaimo** or for a less strenuous walk take the Nº462 bus as far as **Arguayo**, saving an hour of walking and the main 350 metre climb.

Access by car: Car drivers will find plenty of on-street parking around the T-junction in **Tamaimo**.

Our start (and finish) point is the T-junction in **Tamaimo** where the **Los Gigantes** TF-454 road meets the TF-82 main road coming round the mountains from **Guia de Isora**. We begin (Wp.1 0M) by walking south (S) on the TF-82 road, a gentle uphill stroll bringing us to **Calle La Rosa** on our left (Wp.2 3M). Turning left, we climb this steep street, passing **Calle La Ladeira** on the left, to the last house Nº13 at the back of which the tarmac finishes.

We continue on a rough *picon* trail bounded by a rock boulder wall, the bulk of **Montaña del Angel** looming over us on our right, and the peak of **La Hoya** with its antennae away on our left. Old rock walls line the path as we come up a ramp and step over a working water canal (Wp.3 7M), continuing to crunch upwards, the original boulder-laid donkey trail occasionally showing through. Our route swings gently east, flourishing endemic plant life threatening to take over the route (secateurs useful). Swinging right round a Canarian pine brings us to an impressive *mirador*, a good place to get our breath back. Our steady ascent continues between pines, the boulder wall on our left splashed with a white paint boundary marker. The gradient begins to moderate and we look down into a valley populated by a showcase of endemic flora below **Montaña del Angel** on our right as we head up into a bowl in the valley wall. The path widens for a short section before shrubs start to occupy the route; once again, secateurs useful.

Now we face a loose scree, the boulder walls that accompanied us heading off left and right. Ignoring the faint path to the right, we follow the left wall (NE), a faint trail emerging as we progress. Coming to a hole in the wall, we swing right to continue climbing (S) which brings us onto a stone-laid donkey trail which takes us zigzagging upwards, the trail's base disappearing then reappearing briefly, boulder walls to left and right.

Above us, a cave in the slopes of **Montaña del Angel** seems like a portal in a sci-fi movie - or it could be the effects of altitude and exertion! We continue our climb, terrace walls coming into view above us, and **Arguayo** stands out clearly on the ridge behind us. A final *tabaiba*-inhabited slope brings us onto a dirt and rock road where a gentle slope brings us up to the end of a *camino rural* (Wp.4 32M) on top of the ridge alongside the terraces under **Montaña del Angel**.

After that *picon* ascent we take a short detour down the dirt track (S) for impressive views down over **Playa de la Arena**.

Back from sightseeing, we stroll along the *camino* to pass a donkey trail off to our left

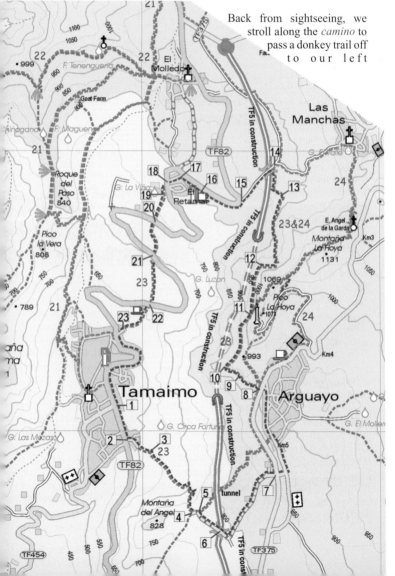

(Wp.5), this is our original route now tunnelled under the new TF-5 road, giving us two alternative routes into Arguayo. We continue along the *camino* to cross the new road on a new bridge (Wp.6) after which we follow the *camino* as it goes left to follow it up to the TF-375 (Wp.7). Now we can either walk up the TF-375; good views but speedy traffic; or cross over onto

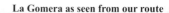
La Gomera as seen from our route

The new road

the old village road turning left at a T-junction to walk up the steep old village main street, passing the closed **Bar El Cercado**, where just after **Taller y Museo Alfarero** we come onto the TF-375 by the bus stop and shelter - our preferred route. Diagonally

left across the road is the continuation of 'True Grit' (Wp.8) going up a steep concrete lane with a staired centre. After all the climbing so far our choice is to take a short diversion by walking up the TF-375 to **Bar Tropic** (230 metres) for some R&R (rest & refreshments) before tackling the next stage. After R&R we stroll back down to the steep concrete lane to use the staired centre for the steep ascent (0M).

Bar Tropic

Views across the Tamaimo valley

When the centre stair finishes, above a triangular *embalse* on our left, we go left onto a walking trail which passes between the terraces (W); continuing up the concrete lane is our 'Lasso La Hoya' route. Our route becomes a boulder-laid donkey trail climbing up the steep slopes below the peak before the gradient moderates (Wp.9). We stroll under sculpted cliffs and then swing north (Wp.10 12M) bringing views across the **Tamaimo** valley and to the knobbly peak of **Roque Blanco**. After an easy stroll, the path changes to rock as we begin energetic climb towards a crest in the trail (Wp.11 19M) before descending gently towards a spur which runs down from the main ridge. The spur ends in a massive rock outcrop, suspended precipitously over the long drop to the valley floor. Large boulder sentinels guard each side of the path as it crosses the spur (Wp.12 24M).

Now the nature of out trail changes as the scar of the TF-5 roadworks dominates the valley below us. We go steeply down towards the valley floor, rich red rock dominating before we reach a section of old gold. Slopes and zig-zags take us down below the spur before the descent moderates beside ancient abandoned terraces (Wp.13) sitting above the new road. We pass a group of pines to swing left (W) and ascend through an S-bend before dropping down to the new pedestrian bridge over the TF-5 (Wp.14). From here our alternative finish and our route, 'Lasso La Hoya' go NE, while we cross the bridge - or more likely, walk across the unmade roadway - to continue on a *picon* track to reach the TF-82 main road at a hairpin bend (Wp.15). Here we have a short stroll down the TF-82 to the service station's bright café with its *mirador* view for a second R&R opportunity (Wp.16).

After a second refreshment stop we walk down the main road to the village of **El Retamar** to turn left down a narrow street (Wp.17) which cuts off the main road's hairpin bend; on meeting the main road (Wp.18) again we cross straight over to go down a tarmac lane, past **Casa de Tejas** (Wp.19), with its noisy dogs, beyond which the lane peters out and we go left onto a narrow walking trail. Although overgrown with grass, this boulder-laid donkey trail is in good condition, bringing us down past a horse and chickens enclosure to cross straight over the main road (Wp.20) to continue steeply down towards **Tamaimo**. Endemic flora flourish as we swing left at a Canarian pine, giving views up to our earlier route below the peak of **La Hoya**, before crossing the main road again (Wp.21), then going left past a small rock outcrop and to concrete and metal water pipes which accompanies our descent between stone walls with its gurgling. A gentle uphill, and the pipe disappears underground before reappearing as we stroll down to the main road (Wp.22) with **Restaurante Vista Guama** a few metres to our right.

Again, we cross straight over the road to follow the donkey trail down past a roofed reservoir where the path is temporarily lost under rock rubble. In a few metres the trail reappears accompanied by two steel water pipes and we walk down to come onto a short street (Wp.23 81M) which brings us into the northern outskirts of **Tamaimo**.

A stroll down the main street provides plenty of opportunities for more refreshments before we reach our start point at the T-juncion with the **Los Gigantes** road. Although the walking time for this route is under three hours (165M), we expect your total time to be significantly longer if you've taken proper advantage of the refreshment stops!

Alternative Finish
From Wp.14 we turn (NE) to walk up to a pine where 'Lasso La Hoya' continues (E) on the dirt track towards **Las Manchas** while we take a track paralleling the new TF-5 road. Approximately half way to the big new roundabout at the end of the TF-5 our track dips down left to pass through a tunnel under the new road. Once we are on the west of the TF-5 our track gradually moves away from the new road for us to strike the TF-375 near its TF-82 junction. From here we have a short stroll along the road to finish in **Santiago del Teide**.

24 LASSO LA HOYA

Our original Lasso La Hoya was a one hour up and down circular that is now our 'Short Option', while our new route takes in the lava landscape below **La Hoya** then climbs to **Las Manchas** where we take a stone-laid *calvario* trail beneath floriferous cliffs before climbing to the **Angel de la Garda** shrine for a mountain top stroll with magnificent views, before deciding between two alternative finish routes. While it is still a 'pocket sized' short route, it encapsulates so much of adventuring in the west of Tenerife this adventure should be included in your itinerary.

Access by car: There is still no sign of the new TF5 road getting finished, so until then take the TF-375 **Arguayo/Santiago del Teide** road off the TF-82 main road . As you come to **Arguayo** the road narrows as it wriggles past **Bar Tropic**, where you should find on-street parking near the bar and recreation area; if there's no parking here, continue higher to the football ground.

Access by bus: the N°462 **Guia de Isora - Los Gigantes** (weekdays only) runs through **Arguayo**. Most convenient departures are 08.00 from **Guia** and 08.50 from **Los Gigantes**. You can combine this route with Walk 23 True Grit to finish in **Tamaimo** with its more frequent bus services.

La Hoya, meaning valley(!), is the sugar-loaf mountain dominating the eastern wall of the **Santiago-Tamaimo** valley. From our start at **Bar Tropic** (Wp.1 0M) we stroll down the

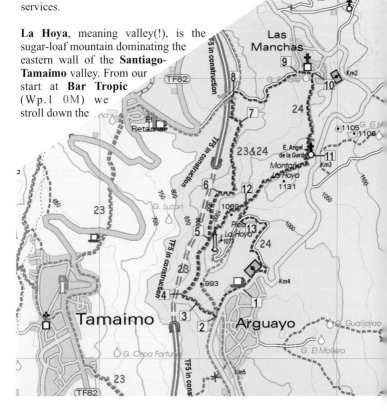

On top of La Hoya

pavement and then the road to meet the route of Walk 23 True Grit (Wp.2 4M) where a steep, stair-centred, concrete lane goes right (W) off the road.

A steep climb brings us to top of the staired centre where our main route goes left (W) on a dirt trail, while our Short Option continues up the last few metres of the concrete.

Short Option

At the end of the concrete a stone-laid trail continues steeply up through cultivated terraces to a small well on the right of our trail. From the well, we take a faint trail going left and right - don't go right onto the terrace where the main trail finishes - to follow a water channel up to a junction of small water canals after which a few more metres bring us up onto the *cumbre*. We continue (NNE) along the *cumbre* on the left of a stone wall and water pipes, to pass a small pylon before coming to a water change point. Continuing alongside a steel water pipe, we duck through the pines keeping left to come onto the access track where it changes from concrete to dirt. Turning left, we head up the track through a hairpin bend to a very steep, centre-staired ascent that brings us up to the end of the concrete track between two transmitter towers.

For our return we take the track downhill continuing on the dirt section from - our upward route through the terraces is easier as an ascent than descent - for a relaxed stroll, meeting our main route coming down a trail on our left (Wp.13) before our track sweeps around a lush bowl before becoming concrete again for its finish at the corner of the football ground and on to the TF-375 where we have a downhill stroll to **Bar Tropic** (Wp.1 approx 60M).

The Main Route

Our trail becomes a boulder-laid donkey trail, climbing the steep slopes before the gradient eases (Wp.3 8M) for us to stroll under wind-sculpted cliffs before swinging north (Wp.4 11M) for views across the **Tamaimo** valley to the knobbly peak of **Roque Blanco**. After an easy stroll, our path changes to rock as we begin an energetic climb towards a crest (Wp.5 18M), where our alternative return joins the main trail - but the faint path is easily missed from this direction. Now it's gently downhill towards a spur running down from the main ridge. The spur ends in a massive rock outcrop hanging above the valley floor, large boulder sentinels stand each side of our trail as we cross the spur (Wp.6 24M).

Below us the scar of the TF-5 roadworks dominates the valley floor as our trail goes steeply down past sections of red and gold rock before our descent moderates beside ancient abandoned terraces standing above the new road (Wp.7). We pass a group of pines to swing left (W) then ascend through an S-bend before dropping down to meet the TF-5 (in construction) at a pedestrian bridge (Wp.8 42M).

- meeting the TF-5 at the pedestrian bridge (Wp.8)

From the eastern side of the bridge a track heads north (our alternative finish in **Santiago del Teide**), while 'True Grit' heads over the bridge (or more likely across the TF-5's incomplete road bed). After a few steps along

Las Manchas Church

the northern track we take a minor track heading up the *picon* slopes of the lava field (E). It's a gruelling ascent on the loose *picon* track as it swings left and then right to head towards **Las Manchas**. Meeting the villages first houses (Wp.9 51M), we continue up onto the village's main street where we turn right to continue climbing steeply up past the church before turning right again (Wp.10 54M) into a cul-de-sac marked by a large wooden cross on a wall.

We are now on the *calvario* though it seems an inconspicuous route until we leave the houses and cultivated plots behind, to come onto a stone-laid trail that runs along the base of a cliff (S). A running water channel burbles alongside our trail beneath a cliff face bedecked in plant life, while on our right the views stretch out over the **Tamaimo** valley with the TF-5 hardly visible. It's a quite delightful path that contours along before crossing the water channel for us to zig-zag steeply upwards on the stone-laid trail, increasing views compensating for our stiff climb, until we emerge beside the TF-375 below the **Angel de la Garda** shrine (Wp.11 63M).

Stepping up to the shrine, we find that behind it a dirt trail leads off through the endemic flora heading around the north-western side of **Montaña La Hoya**; it's an easy trail; remember to stop to take in the spectacular views and plant life. This delightful stroll brings us along to a saddle where the trail splits (Wp.12 74M) giving us a choice of finishing routes.

Easiest finish is to go left to drop down a steep narrow trail, its steepness and stone-littered surface making for a picky descent to the **La Hoya** access track (Wp.13 77M). We go left to follow the track out past the football ground to the TF-375 where a downhill stroll brings us back to **Bar Tropic** (89M).

Going right off the ridge, we also face a steep picky descent with the added challenge of crossing the water channel - I found sitting on the slab, swinging my legs round and jumping down to below the channel a safe if undignified method - before descending onto our outward route (Wp.5 80M) where going left we retrace our outward route back to the road and uphill to **Bar Tropic** (90M).

For this adventure we move away from the dramatic mountains of the west coast and into a gentler landscape of hills and valleys, though there's still plenty of uphill walking as we experience a surprising range of landscapes within two hours. Laurel forests used to cover vast areas of southern Europe and the Canary Islands, but few pockets of these once-mighty *laurisilva* woods remain. The middle section of this route passes through the eerie green stillness of one of these surviving pockets, and the entire route follows dirt roads, paths, *pistas forestales* and tarmac - not a rock climb in sight, resulting in a faster walking pace. With its unique flora, some surreal landscapes and incredible views, this is a route you should not miss.

Access by bus: Reach **Bar/Restaurante Fleytas** on the N°460 bus linking **Playa de las Américas** and **Icod de los Vinos** or the N°360 from **Icod** .

Access by car: Follow the TF-82 through **Santiago del Teide** to continue over the pass to the TF-373 junction. Only use the **Bar/Restaurante Fleytas** car park if you are a customer and have asked permission to leave your car there; otherwise find off road parking on the TF-373.

Our start is at the cheerful **Bar/Restaurant Fleytas**. Leaving the bar (Wp.1 0M), we cross over the road to its southern side and go right to follow the road as it curves through a rock cutting. Just as we come to views down into a bucolic valley, we leave the tarmac on a dirt lane which drops down to our left (Wp.2). We stroll down the lane (W) between bushes of yellow broom with occasional glimpses into the disused quarrying area on our right.

Passing a 'pencil' earth peak, we come down to a bend with views over the lakes and former quarrying area. The lane turns sharp left (S) for us to drop down through zigzags on an easy walking surface, possibly too water eroded for vehicles, until we come to a junction (Wp.3 7M). We go right and then left (Wp.4) to come to a T-junction (Wp.5) where our return route joins us from the left.

We take the dirt road going right, coming to another junction in a few metres (Wp.6 10M) marked by a yellow dot where we go left (W) to another junction (Wp.7) to go right (N), then stay on the main lane as it swings left (W) alongside a dirt wall. After passing a green lane off to our right (Wp.8) we start climbing quite steeply, overlooking fields that now occupy the former stone pits.

Overlooking fields after Wp.8

Climbing to Wp.9

After stopping for a moment (15M) to look back at our route we continue our ascent, the lane climbing steadily up the valley side where white broom has now established itself amongst the yellow in this former quarrying area.

Our upward toil continues, the lane now cutting up through tree-heather covered slopes in a long, steep curve towards the south.

Our *pista* now turns left (SE), the gradient moderating before a hairpin bend (Wp.9 23M) with an unused *pista* ahead as we pass a chain vehicle barrier to continue toiling upward, swinging right (N) below a slope of Canarian pines.

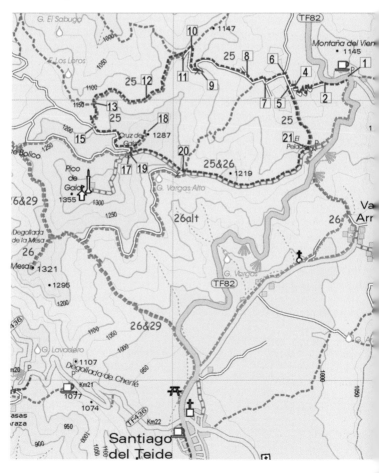

Superb views to Mount Teide

On the final gradient the tree heather on our right gives way, allowing superb views across the valley and to **Mount Teide** which dominates the distant panorama. A final slog brings us onto the top of the ridge (Wp.10 30M), where a trail leads north off our *pista forestal* along the ridge.

For a short diversion, climb the trail to a copse of pines and on as far as a rough rectangular marker post, from where there are fine views over **Erjos**; this trail continuing down towards the village, while we return to the *pista*.

On the ridge (Wp.10) we follow the *pista forestal* south-west up a gentle gradient to large rocks, where the main lane finishes (Wp.11). A rough fire break trail runs up the ridge ahead, as we go right along a narrow path between rocks, immediately after which we enter an ancient, primeval laurel forest.

An easy, springy walking path winds along, climbing gently between mossy banks in this green, Tolkien-like environment. The trail comes up to follow a contour line, the steep slopes above and below us laurel-filled, the path unwinding beneath the high leaf canopy. We stroll through the eerie silence, twisting and turning with the folds in the steep valley wall, the atmosphere mystical. There are no views except for the trail ahead and the forest, and we must follow the path wherever it takes us.

We enter an area of older trees, some dead, marked by dark green, moss-covered boulders both alongside the path and clinging to the slopes above. Then ferns mark a lighter patch in the forest just before we come to a broken tree barring the path (Wp.12 38M note that there is poor GPS coverage on the following section until Wp.13). We duck under and come through a rocky section before the path starts to climb, the forest becoming lighter as we climb from the depths to a crest in the path, then running downhill before swinging back (SW) as we negotiate another broken tree. Glimpses of tree-covered hillsides appear through the forest canopy as we ascend past fallen trees and a mossy outcrop, the path climbing steeply and tree heather replacing the laurels as we approach a junction in the path (Wp.13 44M).

We take the left hand path, climbing steeply over a crest before turning back into the forest again, seeming even darker now after that glimpse of sunshine. We follow the path into a small valley, the trail becoming boulder-laid as it climbs a narrow trench to a junction. The southern route is barred by a pattern of sticks, as we swing west to continue climbing the same narrow defile, the path zigzagging steeply up to a fallen stone marker post at the edge of the forest (Wp.14 50M). Dappled sunlight falls on us as we ascend through tree heathers, passing another marker stone to emerge into the sunshine and onto a *pista forestal* (Wp.15 52M).

We are on the 'wrong', western side of the ridge so we turn left to walk up the *pista* past a stately Canarian pine, and a yellow diamond walking sign pinned to a laurel. The steady uphill becomes steep as we swing up through an S-bend to another yellow diamond on a tree (Wp.16), then continue relentlessly up on this good walking surface until we climb through a bend to a gated and locked junction (Wp.17 60M). Above the junction are large signposts for 'El Pelado, El Saltadero and El Cercado', (the road that we've walked up). On a plinth by the junction is a brass plaque for **Cruz de Gala**, and a north pointer. For a short diversion a path leads up north-east to a heather-covered summit (Wp.18)

From **Cruz de Gala** we squeeze past, or climb up alongside, the locked gates to come down onto the tarmac *camino rural* (Wp.19) which serves the transmitter and forest look-out on the peak of **Mount Gala** to the south-west; a more challenging diversion rewarded with superb views.

Strolling down the tarmac lane, we take in the views over **Valle de Arriba** and **Mount Teide**, and notice the interesting *pista* which runs round the hillside in front of us, an alternative finish on our Walk 26, 'Saddle Up & Round that Mountain' route.

If anything the panoramas improve as we come down the lane, a stark contrast to the atmosphere of the old forest. Far below us, the TF-82 winds up towards the **Puerto Erjos** pass, and we come under an interesting rock outcrop and onto a saddle to get views of our starting point.

Fine views on the downhill section

At the end of the saddle (**Wp.20**) the *pista forestal* runs down the southern slope away from us. Our easy stroll continues down the broad grassy ridge, dropping down through an S-bend to come alongside abandoned terraces, coming onto a small hill before the lane runs downhill again to another small hill. We come to a plinth (Wp.21) on our left signed 'El Pelado' with a north pointer, and just beyond the plaque a traffic sign discourages vehicle access up the lane by a small parking natural area. From **El Pelado** we take the donkey trail dropping down (N) towards the lakes, water eroded in places, for us to meet our outward route at Wp.5, then it's back up the dirt road back to our start point and refreshments in **Bar/Restaurante Fleytas** (Wp.1 115M).

An alternative finish
Continue down the tarmac lane onto the TF-82 and then follow the main road north for a kilometre to the **Los Llanos** junction and the **Bar/Restaurante Fleytas**, an easy downhill alternative finish, but take care to walk on the left side of the main road to face the oncoming traffic.

Breathtaking views combine with a floriferous environment to produce one of the most enjoyable routes in western Tenerife. An energetic start is rewarded by superb flora and exceptional views after climbing onto the saddle at **Degollada de la Mesa**. An ascent onto **Pico de la Mesa**, slightly vertiginous towards the top, brings us the most spectacular views in the region, and that's just the first third of our route. Easy walking takes us out to the **Cumbre de Bolico** and then through the forest to meet our Walk 25, 'Laurel & Hardy' route at **Cruz de Gala**. From the *camino rural* you have an option of a short return on the *pista forestal*, or our route down to **Valle Arriba** and an easy stroll back to **Santiago del Teide** and some well deserved refreshments.

Access by car: Park on the northern edge of **Santiago del Teide** alongside the recreation area, just before the road junction for **Valle de Arriba**.

Access by bus: Service N°460 links **Playa de las Américas** and **Icod de los Vinos** via **Santiago del Teide**; from **Los Gigantes**, take the N°462 or 325.

Our start is north of **Santiago del Teide** just before the **Valle de Arriba** road junction (0M). We stroll alongside the main road with the antennae-topped **Pico de Gala** facing **Pico de la Mesa** across the saddle of **Degollada de la Mesa**, our first destination and yes, it is a long way up! As the main road swings right we step off onto a walking trail originally signed 'Degollada de la Mesa 1h30m' but this has been replaced by a 'dangerous route' sign that we and many other walkers believe to be a spoof by local hunters (Wp.1 5M).

Our narrow donkey trail climbs steadily past a stand of large eucalyptus trees, then as the vegetation thins out we find a small *barranco* on our right. Endemic flora pushes in on our trail as we keep climbing before swinging right to cross the bubbling stream (Wp.2 12M).Now on the stream's northern side, we ascend through tree heather in a series of twists and turns to come onto a rock ledge (Wp.3 18M). It's a relentless ascent, so take rests when you need them, thankfully relieved by expanding views and endemic flora.

An all too brief flat section is replaced by onwards and upwards, the vegetation thinning out as we ascend to another rock outcrop (Wp.4 30M). Small cairns keep us on the trail as it climbs over sections of bare rock for us to come up onto the end of a *pista forestal* (Wp.5 44M) by a small arrow pointing back down our trail.

From the end of the *pista* we take the walking trail heading up towards the saddle, climbing past a rock outcrop (Wp.6 53M) before the final ascent onto the **Degollada de la Mesa** (Wp.7 56M). Views west and south-east from each side of the saddle are impressive, but are as nothing compared to the views coming soon.

From the saddle (0M) our dirt path climbs south-west through the shrubbery, waymarked with green paint. Gradually the path gets steeper and rockier until we turn across the head of a steep *barranco* where trees and plants are bedecked in orange lichen (Wp.9 10M).

Our path becomes slightly vertiginous as we negotiate the final section of climb and scramble to achieve the **Pico de la Mesa** (Wp.10 15M). From this most orogenical and rather vertiginous summit, we have the most spectacular views in the west, if you can bear to look at them! Take care on the descent as both the rock and earth can be slippery and surprise the unwary.

Back on the saddle, there are a number of paths which can confuse walkers

into thinking there is a route up **Pico de Gala**, and their attempts to find a trail makes these false paths more prominent. We look for a green arrow on a rock (0M) and going in its direction, follow a path which becomes a green tunnel of tree heather before becoming a cobbled donkey trail.

On Degollada de la Mesa

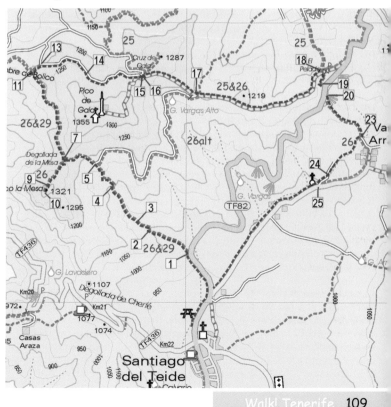

Cobbled descents combine with smooth dirt sections to bring us out into the open with beautiful westward views of rugged mountains, deep *barrancos* and high meadows, the broad path now contouring around the head of the **Barranco de la Madre del Agua** to bring us to a large cairn marking the **El Saltadero** junction of trails (Wp.11 12M).

Views to Teide en route

The main trail continues ahead (W) as we turn right onto a smaller path to climb up through the tree heathers onto a *pista forestal* (Wp.12) where we go right to another junction of trails (Wp.13). Again we turn right to walk up the broad *pista* as it steadily climbs between tree heather.

After the steady climb the gradient eases and **Mount Teide** is picturesquely framed between the tree heathers at one point, then later the red and white antennae on **Pico de Gala** are similarly framed (Wp.14) before we come into a region of poor GPS coverage. Finally we come to the peak of the *pista forestal* for an easy stroll down to the **Cruz de Gala** junction (Wp.15 27M) where we meet our Walk 25, 'Laurel & Hardy' route. Squeezing past the steel gate, we come onto the *camino rural* (Wp.16) for an easy downhill stroll. Below us, a *pista forestal* contours around the slopes and we meet its beginning (Wp.17 35M) to give us a choice of finishing routes:-

(A) Stroll down the *pista forestal* to meet our outward trail at its end, then retrace our outward route down the beautiful valley to the main road (approx. 50 mins)

(B) Our traditional route is to continue down the *camino rural* until it is crossed by a donkey trail at **El Relado** (Wp.18 47M). Going right (S) we are on the remains of a donkey trail for a rough descent in a large zigzag to come onto the main road (Wp.19) after negotiating a new power pole.

Over the road, and in 50 metres we reach the manicured entrance to the donkey trail's continuation (Wp.20); but despite its promise and stone wall, this trail has not been maintained and suffers badly from water erosion, making for a slow descent towards the valley. Some sections are intact (Wp.21) but generally the trail gets worse as we descend with the worst saved for last. Just when you think it can't get any worse, we come to a narrow cutting that drops us down past vine covered terraces on our right to finally emerge at a power pole beside a watercourse (Wp.22 65M).

In wet weather we take the dirt road opposite us (Wp.23) up to **Valle de Arriba** and then follow the road back to our start. In normal conditions we walk along the sandy bed of the water course between stone walls, a stone-laid road joining us from the right (Wp.24) shortly before we come onto the **Valle de Arriba** road just before the church (Wp.25 73M). From here, it's a relaxing stroll through the bucolic landscape back to our start point (85M).

A mixture of donkey trails and paths take us out onto the spectacular ridge which divides **Barranco Seco** from **Barranco de Masca**. 'Spectacular' is often overused, but not in this context as our safe but spectacular, and slightly vertiginous, cobbled donkey trail takes us along the very spine of the ridge for the most impressive *mirador* viewpoints. One choice is to picnic at **Hanging Rock** and return, though energetic hikers will be rewarded for the tough onward route onto the abandoned farmlands of **Guegue**; a true rural idyll protected by fearsome cliffs. Do remember that strolling around the old farmland slopes and descending to view the **Los Gigantes** cliffs has to be paid for on your return ascent. Time and distance is to the top of the **Guegue** sloping plain.

* No refreshments on the route, but **Autobar Cherfe** is almost always open, and a man selling fruit is sometimes parked in the *mirador* parking area.

Access by car: Turn off the TF-82 onto the TF-436 in **Santiago del Teide** signed to **Masca**. You must get out early if you're going to bag a parking place at the *mirador* just above **Casas de Araza** near kilometre marker 20; even on the pass at **Autobar Cherfe** you might have problems parking later in the day!

Alternative start if you've parked at the autobar pass
If you do find yourself parking on the pass, then here is the alternative to walking down the road (boring and none too safe due to disorientated drivers).

Walk behind the autobar, taking the lower grit and dirt path (S) to drop down to a junction (3M) where we take the lower path which turns north and continues downhill to a low boulder wall above abandoned terraces. The path follows the line of the wall south, then north-west to the end of the terraces, from where we go down the slope towards **Casas de Araza**. **Barranco del Natero** drops away on our left as we come down onto a natural rock fence overlooking the farm.

The faintly marked path runs down off the spur towards the houses, bringing us down to an impressive natural rock fence. We go left at the end of the wall, where we find a rock descent to bring us under the face of this unusual outcrop. Impressive views open up all around us as we come down to another outcrop, from where we drop down to pick up a path around the low hill in front of the farm and onto a dirt road.

The farm's noisy (chained) guard dog is more friendly than its owner, who is probably annoyed by those hikers using out-of-date guides and maps to cut through his farm. We follow the dirt road down into a small valley, and then up a stiff climb to the **Masca** road to join our 'official' route.

The start, if you've parked at the *mirador* car park

From the *mirador* car park above **Casas de Aranza** (Wp.1 0M) we walk down the tarmac and step over the chain onto the farm's dirt road (Wp.2).

A path signed 'Finca de Guegue' and marked by stone cairns leads us (W) through willow-like Plocama pendula bushes to a little ridge, then dropping down to a junction where we keep to the right hand path. On this section we overlook the pleasant valley south of us which contains the old route (from when **Casas de Araza** was abandoned).

Mirador **views over Masca**

Our route wriggles its way down the slope (W) to *mirador* views over **Masca**, then zigzags down towards the huge rock wall which forms a saddle at the end of the mountainous ridge. The path divides, then rejoins just before we come onto the saddle (Wp.3 11M), by a white sign with a double-headed black arrow marking the new route (now lying beneath its mounting post), and a line of boulders across the path which comes down from the farm.

A path runs parallel to our route across a valley at the head of **Barranco Seco** on our left (S); part of the infamous 'Forgotten Trail'.

From the signboard, we follow the broad trail over the saddle and start to climb up over rock. Our trail takes us past **Barranco Seco** on the left, which soon becomes a steep canyon.

The donkey trail on the far side (The Forgotten Trail?) starts a precipitous zigzag descent into its depths; meanwhile, our rock-littered path rounds a spur to pass through the remains of a pallet gate (Wp.4), our onward route heading up a boulder-laid 'drawbridge' (Wp.5) towards the ridge ahead.

A climb over gold and then red rock (Wp.6) brings us onto a boulder-laid donkey trail which runs down onto a saddle, with

more *mirador* view down over **Masca**, before climbing another 'drawbridge' to go steadily uphill again surrounded by breathtaking views, then climbing steeply as the well-made trail clings to the sheer walls above **Barranco Seco**, this unprotected sheer drop vertiginous for some walkers.

Looking back to Wp.4

We come away from the sheer drop to climb a sloping red boulder-laid trail, wider here than previously, the gradient moderating to a steady uphill, following stone cairns and faded orange way marking as we climb towards the ridge ahead.

As we ascend, views open up past **Roque Blanco** down the west coast, the tabletop summit of **Roque del Conde** standing out in the distance on a clear day. Over a rock fence, we come onto sheets of gold, red and brown rock to head up to a line of boulders edging our route. Using stone cairns and occasional orange paint for direction, we continue across sheets of rock on the southern side of the ridge.

When we come onto boulder-laid donkey trail the route swings north-west to a saddle between peaks, blood-red boulders lining the route up to a *mirador* (Wp.7 28M) on blood-red rock looking directly down on **Masca**, **Roque Cataño** seemingly insignificant from this altitude. The route reverts to boulder-laid as it swings towards a craggy peak, our broad, sloping trail drawbridge-like as we climb to it (Wp.8).

Once off the 'drawbridge' we lose the **Masca** views, as we steeply ascend the southern face of the peak, coming out onto more sheets of red rock where stone cairns mark the direction, rock-fence remains dividing the sheets into rectangular sections.

Downhill for a short time, then up again on a boulder-laid section to pass a cave (Wp.9). We reach the top of the ridge to climb up past an undercut small peak and onto a rock 'table' on the summit. This is our 'Picnic at Hanging Rock' site (Wp.10 35M), surrounded by stunning geology and breathtaking views.

The first section to 'Hanging Rock' was energetic but now the route becomes seriously energetic, as after dropping steeply down under a giant 'five-fingered hand' of rock (Wp.11 in the heel of the hand) to a steel gravity gate (Wp.12 44M), we face a steep zigzag climb back up onto the ridge (Wp.13) for views down to **Masca**. Our path keeps climbing, steeply at first but then moderating before running along and swinging right (Wp.14 52M) to pass below a trio of caves (Wp.15) before we start another steep zigzag ascent (Wp.16).

At the top of this ascent we come to a corner (Wp.17) featuring decorative small cairns, then a gentle section leads us to another steep climb that brings us onto the top of the ridge again and spectacular views (Wp.19 64M). Our trail crosses to the west of the ridge running under a great hulk of rock, with sheer views on our right, before yet another steep climb brings us up to the summit of our route beside the peak (Wp.21).

Now it's gently downhill with the sloping green meadows and terraces of **Guegue** rolling out in front of us (Wp.22 75M).

On the Guegue plateau

After all that climbing on hard rock, the green meadows and terraces are a welcome relief with colourful chirruping birds flitting amongst the plants, just the place to relax.

A path leads over to the remains of a hut, while lower down the sloping plateau you'll find the remains of houses.

Spectacular views abound from the edges of the plateau, but do remember that there's still plenty of climbing ahead on the return route and exploring down to the old farmsteads will add another 150 metres of ascents to your exertions for the return hike.

Beautiful views from Finca Guegue

Barranco de Masca is Tenerife's second most popular walk after **Barranco del Infierno**, but it's not a favourite with us. It's not because the route is extremely strenuous, vertiginous and potentially dangerous in some sections that we dislike it; it's because it is the only walk on which we've suffered IBS - Irritable Barranco Syndrome! This is a magnificent *barranco* but you can have too much of a good thing, as you'll see on the 'labyrinth' section.

You need to be fully fit to undertake the full route to the beach and back; thus the exceptional 6 walker rating for effort. If your fitness is in doubt, then you can walk down the *barranco* and catch the boat from the beach to **Los Gigantes** (Tel: 922 861918 or 860726 for boat times and bookings before planning your walk).

With its incredible landscape, **Masca** is one location where GPS is not suitable for navigation. The high ridges cut off satellites near the horizon and even with four or five vertical satellites, positional accuracy is poor.

   ** but feels longer   *in **Masca**
We rate the 'downhill only' route finishing at the beach as '4 walker'.

Access by bus: Technically you can catch the N°355 from **Santiago del Teide**, the 10.35 departure normally waiting for the N°460 09.35 departure from **Playa de las Américas** to arrive, but the last bus back from **Masca** is at 16.15 which means that you only have about 5.5 hours to complete the route there and back.

Access by car: Take the TF-436 from **Santiago del Teide**, or **Buenavista** if arriving from the north, and park in the designated area above the village or on approved on-road parking. Start early as these spaces are rapidly filled.

From the road above **Masca** (0M) we walk down into the village on the broad stone-paved walkway, taking the lower path after the church, signed to 'Chez Arlete'. It's steeply down to rejoin the main paved route and walk out onto the southern promontory. Just before we reach **Bar Blanky**, signed 'BAR' on the outside, there are two wooden posts on the left (5M) which mark the start of the walking route. You might like to recover from the twisty drive down to **Masca** in the bar while looking down on the first section of the route.

Stone steps lead us down from the wooden posts and onto the 'path', a clutch of steep, slippery, boot-eroded routes down into the *barranco*. Following the line of a rock 'fence', we skitter down to the palm trees where the path divides, where we take the left hand route to continue steeply down. The paths rejoin and the route becomes a little easier as it winds along the northern side of the *barranco*, a section of stone stairs assisting our descent to abandoned terraces. The massive, sheer-sided bulk of **Roque Catano** looms over us as we come down a stone defile to a 'naturaleza' sign. Our path winds down past large rocks onto an outcrop overlooking a wooden bridge, then a tricky, vertiginous descent brings us down onto the bridge (25M). Across the bridge, a steep climb followed by a narrow path (W) brings us opposite **Roque Catano**, the *barranco* dropping far below us on the right. Walled terraces, some cultivated for grapes, line the southern wall of the canyon as we reach a section where the path narrows dramatically for a vertiginous traverse across a rock slope followed by a scramble, the path then widening to a narrow walking trail as we descend past abandoned terraces and a stone seat under a palm tree. If you're concerned about the nature of the route this far, take a break in this picturesque spot before heading back to **Masca**.

The path narrows after the terraces and drops down steeply to the *barranco* floor which we cross through a dense bamboo thicket. Up past a large rock, we come onto a proper path which makes for relaxed walking as the ravine opens up around us, walled terraces forming a stair on the *barranco* wall as we come to a stone seat, set beneath a shady palm. We now begin a serious descent down rock and boulder slopes to pass under a large rock. The canyon narrows, sheer walls almost closing over us as we descend to the watercourse by a large 'cubist' boulder. We continue downhill on the northern side of the watercourse to curve under a huge boulder, a steep descent on boulders polished by hikers' boots. After this narrow defile, the *barranco* opens out as we come below veined cliffs on polished rock sheets towards a low dam wall. Across the watercourse, we continue down to the 'plain' where another ravine joins us from the north (59M).

Before stepping over the canal at the left of the dam wall and taking the steps down to the *barranco* floor, take a moment to appreciate the beauty of this area, as ahead of us lies the 'labyrinth'. Our path, marked by the brown scuffing of boots, meanders down the floor of the *barranco* as it narrows. Massive chunks of rock dam the defile in this section, and we go under the first of these rock falls, beneath an upended cone of rock (watch out for the large hole alongside the path, big enough to swallow the largest hiker). We scramble down and then across the *barranco* floor to another rock fall. Steeply down the escarpment beside a photogenic waterfall and pool, we then meander across the stream to climb up, following the tortuous route of the defile. Sheer rock walls fly up hundreds of metres above us as we follow the path, marked by a small cairn of stones, to the unlikely sight of a fence. The ravine turns through ninety degrees, and we curve round a large rock to the even more unlikely sight of a green and yellow metal gate, propped open across our path. Again we drop down to the grey pebble *barranco* floor as the path takes us over the watercourse.

Ahead, sunlight streams into the *barranco* where it widens. It's steeply down across another rock fall blocking the ravine, crossing the floor again to yet another giant rock fall. This descent is more like caving as we emerge below the fall, to walk down past a stone stair which leads up to the water canal built in the southern wall. Down two more rock falls, we eventually reach a sunlit rock promontory (100M). Though it seems as if we must be nearing the sea, this is a false dawn. As the ravine widens, another one joins us from the north, creating an airy sunlit area in contrast to the narrow defile we have just come through. We realise that there's still a lot of *barranco* to go before we reach the sea, and are hit by an attack of IBS!

As you begin to appreciate the nature of this *barranco*, you won't be surprised to find the defile twisting this way and that below immense sheer walls, giant rock falls often with scrambling descents the norm rather than the exception.

Often, the path divides and we often seem to pick the most difficult route. Rather than give a step-by step commentary of the journey through this surreal landscape, we urge you to stay on the path. If you come to a seemingly impossible descent, then you have probably taken the wrong route when the path last divided, so backtrack and follow the alternative path. Use the small cairns of stones where they exist, and don't be surprised by steep climbs and descents as these do occur on the

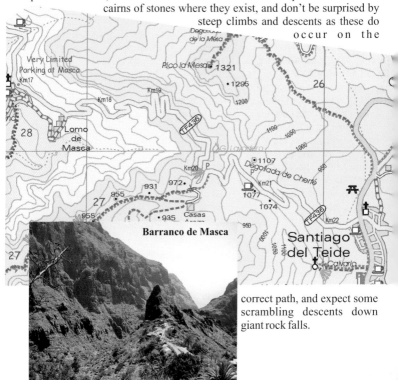

Barranco de Masca

correct path, and expect some scrambling descents down giant rock falls.

Just as you think that this seemingly endless ravine will go on for ever and after several attacks of IBS, we come to the hopeful sign of abandoned terraces on the southern wall (155M). After zigzagging down the terraces and scrambling onto the floor, we climb up the rocks to a turn in the *barranco*. There's blue sky ahead! In our excitement we take the wrong trail along the *barranco* floor, including a 'slide and jump' descent through a massive rock fall. We stagger across the large pebble rocks to reach the beach (174M).

Families of friendly cats share our lunch as we relax on this bay enclosed by sheer cliffs with its single holiday home. Several tourist excursion boats call in, their occupants lurching about on deck or jumping into the sea. If you pre-booked a boat ride to **Los Gigantes**, take the walkway out to 'pimple island' and join the crowd awaiting a sea-borne release.

Our return (0M) to **Masca** is tougher than the descent as we face a strenuous 550-metre climb in altitude. After R & R, we set off on the return journey, following a steel water pipe up the south side of the *barranco*, to bring us onto abandoned terraces which bypass our 'slide and jump' descent of our downward route. However, our descent from the terraces is a scramble down a rock wall just past the rock fall, followed by a slippery traverse across rock sheets and back onto our downward route. This path is easily missed when coming down the *barranco*.

Well into the labyrinth, we take a break (35M), having already climbed high up the northern wall. We take another break (61M), the *barranco* echoing in various languages, 'How much further is it?' from those on the downward route. We reach the stone stair up to the water canal (89M) and then avoid the 'slide and drop into a pool'(105M) by taking the path up the south side of a huge rock fall. Past the dam, and we sink thankfully onto the stone seat under the palm (120M), the abandoned terraces reminding us that we are not too far from the village.

We reach another stone seat under a palm (131M) at the top of the lawned terraces, and soon after (141M) the village of **Masca** comes into sight, high up and far away, as we take care on the vertiginous sections of the path, reaching the wooden bridge (146M). The section after the bridge is the steepest part of our return. We labour upwards, inspired by survival instinct and the sight of **Bar Blanky** high above us. These grit slopes are as potentially treacherous uphill as down, but we emerge between the wooden posts onto the paved walkway having taken almost exactly the same time as on our downward route (170M).

On the wooden bridge

In one minute more, we totter into **Bar Blanky**, the *agua con gas* tasting unbelievable good, where we ponder our new attributes as stegophilists.

Spectacular ridge-top *mirador* views are our reward for slogging up the 300 metre ascent at the start of this Western Classic route, followed by an easy descent to the **Mirador Café** at **Cruz de Galdor** overlooking **Masca** village with a final trail descent to **La Vica** from where it's a road stroll to the famous village.

I've researched the route for car drivers parking at **Santiago del Teide** while bus users (Titsa N°460 service) could opt for an even more varied day out by starting at **Bar/Rest Fleytas** to follow Walk 25 to Wp.15 or Wp.17 and then linking to our main route at Wp.6 or Wp.9. Return from **Masca** on the spectacular N°355 bus service at 16.15; the N°460 service always waits at **Santiago** to link with the N°355 service.

If you'd prefer a longer route than **Masca** then you can continue on from Wp.15 following the 'Teno Alto' trail down the ridges to finish at **Buenavista** and catching the 15.45 N°355 bus for the full ride through **Masca** and back to **Santiago del Teide**.

Since we first researched this route the 'official' sign shown below has been removed to be replaced by a 'dangerous route' sign; see also Walk 26. There is no difference to the trail in this conversion from 'official' to 'dangerous', this being confirmed to the many walkers we have talked to, so we assume the 'dangerous route' sign is a spoof erected by local hunters.

We start out from the café picnic area just north of the church (Wp.1 0M) to stroll along the **Icod** (TF82) road, passing the **Valle Arriba** junction and when

Wp.2-the original 'official' sign

the road swings right we step off onto a signed trail (Wp.2 7M see left and above). Our trail heads up the side of a steadily steepening *barranco*, crossing the watercourse (Wp.3) to the northern side where the trail steepens.

Looking back to Valle Arriba

It's a steady slog onwards and upwards, with small cairns guiding us across the rock sections before we emerge onto the end of a *pista forestal* (Wp.4 40M). Our rocky onward trail is signed off the end of the *pista* for a steep climb up to the top of the ridge where we step out onto the **Degollada de la Mesa** (Wp.5 55M) - see Walk 26 if you want to climb **Pico de la Mesa**.

Views from the *degollada* are spectacular, massively more spectacular if you follow Walk 26 up **Pico de la Mesa**, but unfortunately the summer 2007 forest fires have devastated the tree heather as we follow the trail (green paint waymark) down off the *degollada* to start contouring around the massive bowl at the head of **Barranco de la Madre de Agua**.

At Wp.4

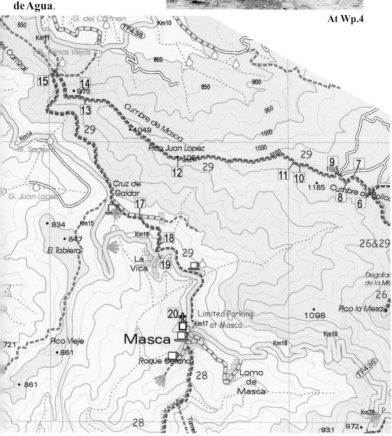

Our broad trail contours around to bring us to the cairn marking the **El Saltadero** junction (Wp.6 67M; Walk 26 Wp.11) where Walk 26 goes right up the narrower trail.

We continue straight ahead on the main trail, an easy earth path amongst tree heathers bringing us along to the strange sight of 'mesh nets' apparently strung to collect condensation (Wp.7 71M) just before our trail drops down to a *mirador* viewpoint (Wp.8). We drop down the trail to a signed junction 'Puerto de Erjos 1h, Las Portelas 1h' on a broad *pista forestal* (Wp.9 74M).

Turning west, we stroll across the grass saddle past a ruin to the trail signed 'Teno Alto'. We're into tree heather, fire damaged on the west, as we make our way along the ridge, our route widening (Wp.10) before coming to a path junction (Wp.11 76M) where we keep right to drop down the northern slope in a steep descent before the gradient eases for us to emerge from the tree heather onto the top of the ridge before dropping down again on a picky descent to emerge on a mirador viewpoint (Wp.12 97M) overlooking the

The Teno Alto sign after Wp.9

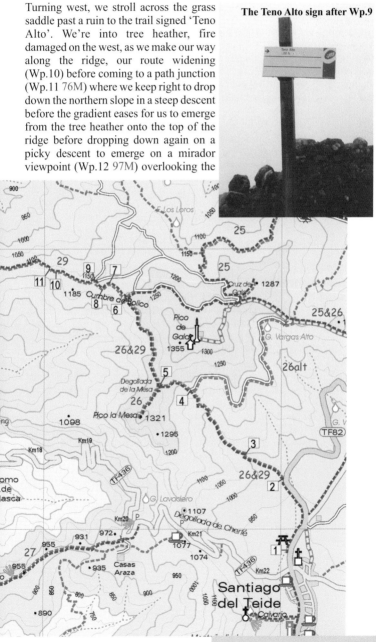

Masca village and *barranco*.

Continuing along the ridge trail we are again in green 'tree heather' tunnels (poor GPS reception) as we descend along the northern face before emerging onto another western viewpoint (Wp.13 115M) where we can almost see the **Mirador Café** on **Cruz de Galdar**, the **Masca** road now invitingly near below us.

Another descent on the northern face of the ridge is followed by crossing a small saddle onto the western face (Wp.14 120M). Now we are heading away from the café, still descending to skitter down onto a saddle with a four-way trail junction (Wp.15 126M); ahead is 'Teno Alto, 4h', the long distance alternative to finish in **Buenavista**, back right is 'Martin Bau', while left, 'Cruz de Hda', is our onward trail.

Our trail swings left (SE) for an easy descent below our earlier route as we contour along beneath the ridge on a broad donkey trail supported by rock walls, the valley below us coming slowly up to join us as we finally go down a paved slope to join the **Masca** road behind the **Mirador Café** (Wp.16 147M) on the **Cruz de Galdar**; note the small lane (*camino rural*) just north of the café - our onward route.

It would be a crime to ignore this ideally situated refreshment stop. In good weather enjoy a *café con leche* on the terrace while drinking in the views down to **Masca** village before setting off on our final stage.

From the **Mirador Café** (0M) we take the *camino rural* serving a pair of houses and shortly before reaching the houses we drop off the tarmac onto a walking trail (Wp.17 2M) to start a picky descent down through small, mostly abandoned, terraces. A spring running across the trail makes for a soggy section after which its all steadily downhill on the narrow path until it runs out onto a paved track (Wp.18) that drops us down into the hamlet of **La Vica**, joining the **Masca** road by the **Bar/Rest Masca** (Wp.19 15M). Turning left we have a downhill stroll on the tarmac, keep a watch out for the 'white-knuckled' hire-car drivers, before passing a restaurant entrance for the final uphill to the entrance to **Masca** village and the bus stop (Wp.20 25M).

Bus N°355 leaves **Masca** at 16.15 so depending how quickly you have completed the route you could find yourself with plenty of time with which to explore the start of the **Barranco de Masca**, rummage round the shops specializing in tourist gewgaws, taking refreshments in the bars and restaurants, or possibly strolling along the walkway (*camino rural*) to the museum at **Lomo de Masca**. Just don't forget to be on time for that 16.15 bus!

30 MONTAÑA MAJÚA - TOFFEE MOUNTAIN

Las Cañadas is a big crater with the emphasis on BIG. Just drive from **Boca Tauche** to **El Portillo** to see how big this region is. It's just as big on foot, but being in direct touch with this amazing landscape means that the visual illusions are greater. In **Las Cañadas** everywhere looks closer than it is; in fact much closer, as your eyes foreshorten the large distances. Look at **Mount Teide** - it seems as if you could just reach out and touch it! **Toffee Mountain**, or **Montaña Majúa**, is our introduction to walking in these high altitudes (2000+ metres) and if our description tends towards describing the scenery in confectionery terms then blame it on the thin air.

Whether arriving by bus or car, we recommend that you take a ten to twenty minute break when arriving at this altitude to let your body acclimatise before starting walking.

3 | 3H | 13.5 km | 200m / 200m | ↻ | 1*

* at the **Parador** café

Access by car: Take the TF-21 to **Las Cañadas**. The park authorities have closed off access to the dirt *pistas* such as **Siete Cañadas** which used to provide a lot of car parking, thus putting increased pressure on the **Mirador Ruleta** car park and the small amount of road side parking near the **Parador Café**.

Access by bus: N°342 from **Playa de las Américas** and **Los Cristianos** or N°348 from **Puerto de la Cruz** will take you to the **Parador**, from where you wander over to our start point at the café terrace. There's only one departure and return of these routes each day, so make sure you don't miss your bus!

From the café, we walk past the hotel entrance and set off down the access road. Keeping an eye to our right, we spot the start of 'sendero 19' (Wp.1 3M) signed at the start of a narrow walking trail. We are heading east towards a 'caramac' coloured lava flow, passing two more *sendero* signs nailed to rocks, after which our trail becomes less distinct in the broken ground. Small stone cairns keep us on route to reach more *sendero* signs (Wp.2 11M) before meeting the original path coming in from the right (Wp.3 13M) as we come up to the 'caramac' lava wall.

Now the original and new routes have come together, we follow the narrow trail as it skirts the lava wall (N). More 'S19' signs are followed by twin S19s (Wp.4 20M), confirming our route as we leave the first lava wall behind to cross a plain towards another lava flow. Coming below the lava (Wp.5), more toffee than caramac this time, and another S19, we skirt this new lava flow. It's an easy stroll to come between two large rocks (S19 Wp.6) before passing a possible path off to our left, then coming to an interestingly veined rock on the right of our path (Wp.7 30M), seemingly a laminate of various rocks.

Our sandy path, rather like dune walking, moves out from the lava wall for a while before curving back guided by small cairns towards an obsidian finger of rock (Wp.8) followed by more 'S19' signs. More small cairns guide us as the 'crunchy bar' coloured mound of **Montana Majúa** comes into view, with a small valley on our right. We come into a broken landscape of spiky rock outcrops before walking up a water runoff (Wp.9), cairns again confirming our route in the direction of the cable-car station. The small valley end sas we come up to a 'Peligro Colmenas' (danger - beehives) sign (Wp.10 56M), then pass a second sign on our right. On our right is a small ridge which runs up to **Montaña Majúa** as we go right (Wp.11) to climb across the open 'crunchy bar' ground onto the line of the ridge to find a *sendero* (Wp.12) heading up towards the rounded peak.

We make no excuses for our slow progress up the steep trail, the thin atmosphere requiring a number of breaks before we reach the trig point (Wp.13 71M and 2353 metres altitude on our GPS).

From the trig point of 'toffee mountain' (0M) we go gently uphill (NE) to pass piles of lava stones as we cross the peak, then come onto a faint walking trail which drops down towards the **Pista Sanatorio**.

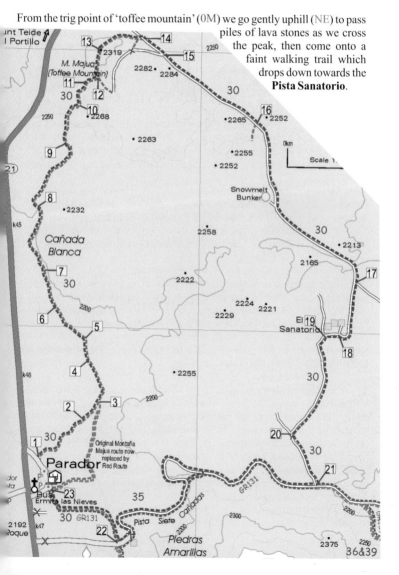

Before descending, the roofs of the **Sanatorio** are visible away to the south-east, our next destination. We come down the trail, passing a path off to our right (Wp.14 6M) as we come onto the *pista* and 'S16' sign to walk past a junction where another *pista* goes off to our right. **Pista Sanatorio** has a good walking surface, allowing us to make relaxed progress while taking in the subtle colourations of the rock formations in this region. Three strange metal covers (Wp.15) are passed on our left as we bowl along the dirt road to pass a path off to our right (Wp.16 17M) just before our route curves right to run gently downhill. We come down to a strange sight at a junction where a bunker appears to have been concealed in a rock mound (S16 22M). If you take a couple of minutes to walk up to the locked door you'll see that the 'bunker' contains the large pipes of the system used to capture the snow-melt off **Mount Teide**; those metal covers are also part of this water system.

At the Samatorio

Leaving the 'bunker' behind, we stroll along past another 'S16' sign before passing a *pista* off to our left (S16s and Wp.17). The **Sanatorio** roofs come into view on our right just before our *pista* curves between large rocks to the **Sanatorio** entrance (Wp.18 45M), just the place for a pleasant break after that power walking.

From the **Sanatorio** (0M), we continue on the *pista*, passing a path and a track off to our right (Wp.19), the **Las Cañadas** cliff wall rising ahead of us. An easy stroll brings us past a *pista* to the right (Wp.20) to negotiate a metal barrier across the main *pista* - hurdle over if tall enough, or duck under - before we come down to the route of our Walk 37, 'Siete Cañadas' (Wp.21 15M) alongside the cliff wall.

If you're looking at your GPS in this location, you might notice it producing strange readings. The vertical escarpment cuts off satellite reception to the south, giving unreliable readings; not that you need any navigation devices for the next stage, along the **Siete Cañadas** *pista* heading west.

We join this walking motorway of **Las Cañadas** for an easy stroll as it climbs and twists along below **Montaña Guajara**, ascending until we reach a left curve with panoramic views down over the **Parador**. Then it's downhill as the *pista* curves left and then right, passing a path before coming to the vehicle barrier (45M) just before the tarmac starts. In our relaxed stroll down the tarmac it's all too easy to miss the narrow path off to the right (Wp.22) that leads to the **Parador**. Leaving the tarmac, we follow the faint trail across the lava to come onto a little-used *pista* which we follow westwards until we come to a path off to our right. This path leads us up to the **Las Cañadas** notice board (Wp.23) on the south side of the **Parador**, and in a few more metres we're back at our starting point on the café terrace, three hours (180M) from the beginning of our walk.

31 BLACK SAND SURPRISE - ARENAS NEGRAS

High mountains mean big views and few routes come close to this combination of easy walking with magnificent views to be experienced on our **Arenas Negras** route from the **Visitors' Centre** at **El Portillo**. We climb 200-plus metres, but it happens so gently that you hardly notice; the views expand and expand, and if that isn't enough, the ground opens at our feet into a great chasm. Skitter down the side of a black sand cliff, and we have a terrific introduction to the excitements of **Las Cañadas**.

Access by bus: N°342 from **Playa de las Américas & Los Cristianos**, N°348 from **Puerto de la Cruz**; there's only one departure and return of these services each day, so make sure you don't miss your bus!

Access by car: Park at the **Visitors' Centre** car park opposite the start of our route; usually plenty of spaces.

The start of the route

We start from the extensive parking area at the **Visitors' Centre** close to **El Portillo**. Across the road (Wp.1 0M) we go past the barrier on the **Siete Cañadas** dirt *pista* to cross a shallow valley before coming up to a junction of *pistas* (Wp.2 5M) where we go left (*sendero* 2) on the minor *pista*.

After taking the track at Wp.2

It's a gentle ascent (ENE) in amongst the tundra, a soft landscape compared to much of **Las Cañadas**, on what was once a dirt road though since no-one has driven this route for years, nature is gradually reclaiming it. Our *pista* swings right (Wp.3 13M) to head south before swinging back east north-east and gradually narrowing to walking trail width (Wp.4 26M) hemmed in by bushes of Teide broom (Spartocytisus supranubius).

Below us, the scenic TF-24 road crosses the high *cumbre* to **La Laguna** as views ahead open up over the **Orotava Valley** and **Puerto de la Cruz**, the **Los**

Realejos *cumbre* looking particularly impressive from our elevated position (Wp.5). Our path is climbing very gently, almost contouring around **Montaña Arenas Negras** and bringing the top of the **Izana** observatory into view just before pushing through bushes of Teide broom which try to overwhelm the path (Wp.6).

After the easy contouring, our path starts a steady ascent (SE) to bring us up to a hairpin bend (Wp.7 48M) where confused walkers have created short false paths, giving the impression of a trail junction. Keeping right, we continue ascending through more broom to a second hairpin bend (Wp.8 56M) by large rocks and a small cliff. More of the **Izana** observatory comes into view as we traverse the lower slopes of **Montaña Arenas Negras**, gradually swinging south (S) as we climb.

Our route curves as we ascend between **Arenas Negras** and **Cerrillar** mountains, the climb gradually easing so that we are hardly aware of reaching the high point of our route as the magnificent panorama of **Mount Teide** comes into view.

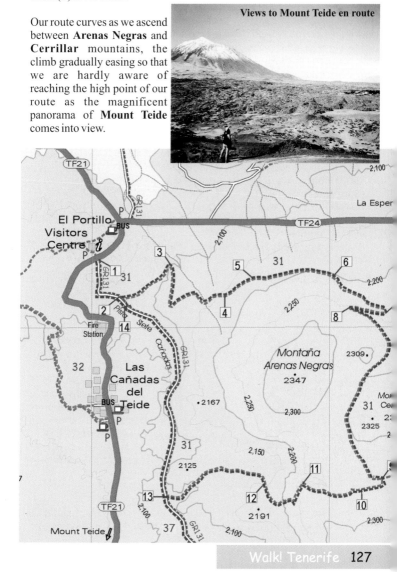

Views to Mount Teide en route

Now we are back to easy strolling as our trail widens allowing us to take in the panoramas as we progress. We gradually curve south-east to come to a junction (Wp.9 80M) where the path ahead with a line of rocks across it heads towards the *cumbre*, while a *sendero* marker (2) directs us right (W) on a faint trail.

There are small cairns and another *sendero* marker (Wp.10) guiding us into a gully which opens into a great chasm at our feet, as more *sendero* markers guide us left along the southern side of the canyon to bring the **Las Cañadas del Teide** restaurants into view (Wp.11 88M).

If the canyon was a surprise, we immediately come to another as our path takes us onto a black *picon* mountain, our route coming back to the canyon's edge before sweeping left across the steep black slope in a skittering descent to large rocks. Below the rocks, the path is steeper as we zigzag down the black slopes as slowly as practical to keep a sure footing, before the path runs off the slopes down a small gully to a *sendero* marker (Wp.12 105M). Our route steepens for another skittery descent on black *picon* before coming down to the floor of **Las Cañadas**, the black mountain and giant canyon dominating the landscape behind us.

The valley floor makes for easy walking, but the path is very faint as we head east along the left side of a valley, *sendero* markers keeping us on track until our route runs out to meet the **Siete Cañadas** *pista* (Wp.13 118M). Turning right (N) we stroll along the *pista*, which is pleasant enough, though nothing like as exciting as our earlier route, passing *sendero* signs and a short stiff ascent before reverting to easy strolling.

More easy strolling takes us past *sendero* markers and a vehicle barrier (Wp.14) before meeting our outward route at the *pista* junction (Wp.2 138M) and then up to the main road (143M). You can savour this route a second time by driving up to the most southerly of the overpriced **Las Cañadas** restaurants, from whose terrace you have superb views across to that skittering black *picon* mountain descent, and the huge canyon that we nearly stepped into.

La Fortaleza's red cliffs are one of Tenerife's classic high altitude walking routes. Views are spectacular from the peak of **La Fortaleza**, from the western end of the **La Fortaleza** massif, and from the **Riscos de La Fortaleza**, all of which are covered in this route. On a map the route looks straight forward, but the broken ground of **Las Cañadas** combined with the 2000+ metre altitude make it demanding, energy sapping yet rewarding.

Access by bus: N°342 from **Playa de las Américas** & **Los Cristianos**, N°348 from **Puerto de la Cruz**; there's only one departure and return of these services each day, so make sure you don't miss your bus!

Access by car: Park off the road at the southern end of the **Las Cañadas del Teide** restaurants.

Our start point is at the southern end of **Las Cañadas del Teide** where we park near the **Bar/Rest Bamby** (Wp.1 0M). After walking north past the bar, we turn left onto a dirt road (Wp.2) with a *Peatonal* sign.

The dirt road peters out behind the bar into a well-trodden gravel path (Wp.3 3M) and in a few metres we pass a branch of the path (Wp.4) heading back towards the settlement. It is a surreal experience walking on this manicured path through the broken land of the **Cañadas** with Teide broom (Spartocytisus supranubius) pushing in on our route.

A few minutes into the route

After fifteen minutes the gravel ends (Wp.5 15M) and we continue on a traditional dirt path amongst spewings of rock, meandering through valleys towards the peaks of **La Fortaleza** and **El Cabezón**, seen from the crests of our route.

Dropping into a steeper valley, we cross its water course (Wp.6 21M) to climb up past a piece of manicured path to come to a junction with a stone seat (Wp.7 25M), where 'sendero 6' is signed left to **Mount Teide**. In another four minutes we pass the path of *sendero* 6 (Wp.8 29M) signed right to **El Portillo**, and an alternative start for the **La Fortaleza** route.

Views open up on our right as we climb steadily through the broken land to pass a 'sendero 1' marker (Wp.9 38M) near the edge of the pine forest before swinging westwards. On past a weather station on our right, our route comes through a 'rock gateway' with a 'sendero 1' sign (Wp.10 43M), to head north-west to reach the top of a slope overlooking the gravel plain below **La Fortaleza** (Wp.11 48M). At the bottom of the rough path we come onto the plain (Wp.12) to head towards the *degollada*.

The gravel plain becomes a steep sand beach, making the climb up towards the pass doubly difficult until the sand gives out. We finish the ascent on a conventional dirt and rock path, passing a path off to our left (Wp.13 65M), then reaching the small *ermita* and **Cruz de Fregel** recreation area set on the *degollada*. **Cruz de Fregel** was burnt down during the forest fires and is due to be rebuilt so you may find a new picnic area and *choza* but this work had not been started on our latest visit.

From the *choza* (0M) we take a dirt road north-west which climbs gently past a small memorial shrine (Wp.14) before it finishes in open ground north of the **Fortaleza** peak (Wp.15 6M). Clear paths go straight ahead and to the left, which we take to steadily ascend (S) to the peak (Wp.16 14M) and superb views.

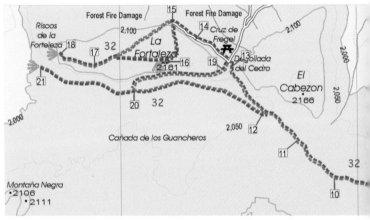

From the summit a new curved path takes us westwards to join our original path shortly before an interesting rock formation (Wp.17) to come above the cliffs, continuing past a small peak before running out into an eroded gully (Wp.18). It's possible for the foolish and adventurous to scramble down the gully, then going left to meet our later route at Wp.21, but this is not for us. The best views are back at the small peak before retracing our route back to the *choza* on the *degollada*.

Our second leaving of the *degollada* (0M) is on the main trail (SW), passing our inward route (Wp.13), and swinging right (Wp.19). The route narrows to a small path with Teide broom pushing in on our route as we stroll along beneath the impressive cliffs of **La Forteleza**. This once used to be a dirt road but is now hardly a walking route in places as nature and erosion reclaims the land; secateurs are useful.

Careful footwork is necessary before we come down to the edge of the plain where cairns mark the route out to a junction of paths (Wp.20 12M). Turning west, we follow the trail out to the **Riscos de la Fortaleza** (Wp.21 22M) for the impressive views out over the pine forest to the **Teno** mountains and the north-west coast of Tenerife.

Superb views from La Fortaleza

It's time to head back to base, retracing our steps to the edge of the grit plain and taking the general path across this strange phenomenon back to our entry point (Wp.12). A stiff climb up the eroded trail takes us back into the broken land of the **Cañadas**. Again, this region of valleys, descents and ascents is tougher than it looks on the maps as we retrace our steps.

Passing the *sendero* 6 junctions (Wps. 8 & 7) we're glad not to be tackling **Teide** on foot in this thin atmosphere, as we slog through this difficult landscape to arrive

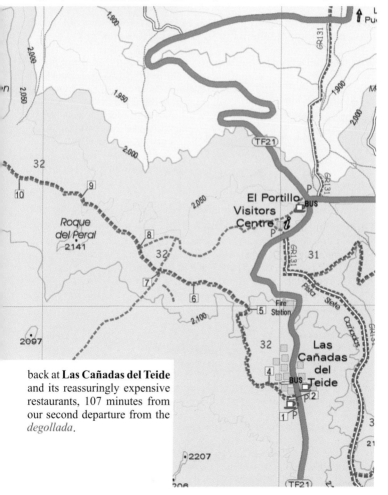

back at **Las Cañadas del Teide** and its reassuringly expensive restaurants, 107 minutes from our second departure from the *degollada*.

Walking routes don't have to be excessively long or strenuous to be spectacular. **Roques de García** is an accessible classic, within most peoples easy compass. Spectacular geology gives an interesting viewpoint on the **Las Cañadas** region in a compact tour. If there is a criticism, it's that this route is so accessible that you may find it crowded with other walkers. Walk the route in the direction we take, as the reverse direction involves a descent from the **Mirador de la Ruleta**, where boot erosion makes for a slippery, potentially hazardous, steep descent; much easier to climb than descend.

3 1¼H 4 km 140m / 140m 1

Access by bus: N°342 from **Playa de las Américas** & **Los Cristianos**, N°348 from **Puerto de la Cruz**; there's only one departure and return of these services each day, so make sure you don't miss your bus!

Access by car: Parking in the National Park is quite restricted so it is best to arrive early (before 11.00am) at the large **Mirador Ruleta** car park.

From the *mirador* roundabout, viewing paths lead up to the left and right - not part of our route - to give spectacular views down over the **Llano de Ucanca** plain and lava fields. We start from the north of the roundabout (Wp.1 0M), following the well-trodden path between roped-off *naturaleza* areas for a pleasant stroll to come below the impressive and much photographed, **God's Finger** (Wp.2) on our left, the huge clumps of rock on our right resembling building foundations.

Our path curves left (Wp.3) - with an option to go left to a viewpoint over the **Ucanca** plain - becoming very rocky as we pass another ridge on our left to come under cliff walls before another viewing point on our left (Wp.4). The rocky surface

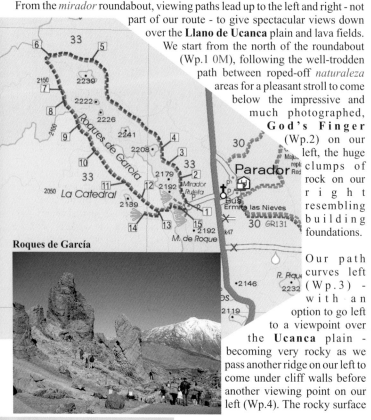

Roques de García

gives way to grey sand as we head north-west to a pass between a lava field on our right and the impressive rock formations on our left.

A short climb brings us up under the rocks and alongside an area of dark grey 'hippo-backed' lava field on our right before curving left around rock pinnacles to face a large wind-sculpted rock formation (Wp.5 17M); the wind erosion having carved 'cartoon heads' of rock on its southern face. We pass a 'sendero 3' marker and come onto a lava field before coming under the mass of rock for our path to run down its northern side. Cairns both sides of the path (Wp.6 21M) mark the start of our descent down towards the plain, the loose rock-and-scree path making for a slow, picky descent, a remarkable 'tree root' system of knotted lava becoming visible on our right where it has solidified in the midst of tumbling down between the rock pinnacles.

Finally, the scree-covered path descent ends at the start of another hippo-backed lava field (Wp.7), making for easier progress.

Past an 'S3' sign, small cairns give guidance across the lava sheet as we overlook the **Ucanca** plain (Wp.8) and pass examples of Teide wallflower (Erysimum scoparium) before moving across to the east of the lava field (Wp.9).

Crossing the lava field

We come under buttress-like rock projections, the self-shattering pillars soaring surreally skywards, before reaching the end of the hippo-backed lava and coming onto a plain (Wp.10 45M).

Now it's an easy stroll along the grey sand path towards the 'Cathedral', a Gaudiesque volcanic creation rising over one hundred metres out of the plain, passing an 'S3' marker (Wp.11 50M) as we come under the great rock. Keeping left, we past east of the 'La Catedral' and our path starts a gentle ascent to pass a 'S3' marker (Wp.12), then climbing with a bit more urgency on this long slogging ascent, so pace yourself. There are several routes, first up to the saddle and then up to **Mirador de la Ruleta**, but we keep with the most climbed route, passing a boulder and cairn before coming up alongside the saddle on our right. We take a dirt path (S) to the saddle (Wp.13 59M) and then on to the *mirador* (Wp.14) by a 'mosaic' rock outcrop overlooking the **Ucanca** plain.

Coming back from the *mirador*, we take a higher dirt path back onto the main climb. The route splits frequently now, but we take the steepest uphill route at each option on grit-covered slopes that would make a tricky descent. Voices come down to us from above - not a holy experience but crowds of WI- style tourists released from their coaches line the **Mirador de la Ruleta** above us. Climbing the most energetic section of our route under their watchful eye is rather unnerving, so it's a bit of a disappointment not to be cheered as we spring over the parapet onto the *mirador* (Wp.15 75M).

Paisaje Lunar's unique 'moonscape' geology is one of Tenerife's classic routes which should be on all walkers 'must do' list. The basic route **(A)** is a straightforward 45 minutes each way, while our route takes an eastern return route via **Campamento Madre del Agua** revealing a more varied landscape (two hours walking). There's also the option of walking in from the TF-21 junction **(B)** just above km.66 (6.5kms and 90 minutes each way). For mountain bikers and four-wheel drivers wanting a challenging route, or for masochistic walkers wanting a full day in the heights above **Vilaflor**, we include a brief description of the **Agua Agria** *pista forestal* **(C)** which takes in unusual rock formations and the spectacularly sited 'dead tree' *mirador*.

The refurbished **Pista Madre del Agua** provides easy driving (20kmh speed limit) access to our 'official' start at Wp.8 but please park responsibly as this is technically a public road. The vehicle barrier, just off the TF-21, is unlocked as we go to press but may be subject to closure by the forestry authority.

(A) Basic circular walk 3 walker; **(B)** from TF-21 and return 4 walker; **(C)**TF-21 to **Paisaje Lunar** and **Pista Agua Agria** 5 walker

Access by car: if the **Pista Madre del Agua** vehicle barrier is closed the nearest parking is at **Big Pine Mirador** opposite the forestry house above **Vilaflor**; see map section.

(A) From Pista Madre Agua to the start of the Main Walk

Our start point is above **Vilaflor** on the TF-21 just past the km.66 marker where we turn off the main road at the hairpin bend onto a broad *pista forestal* (Wp.1). Setting the odometer to zero, we set off along the dirt road, passing a path off to the left and a chained private *pista* to the right, then a ruined cottage on our left at 2.4km (Wp.2). We pass the barred *pista* to **Galeria El Pino** at 3.2km (Wp.3) after which we go downhill to cross the water course of **Barranco de la Mesa** shortly after which the **GR131** crosses the pista; here we have an option to follow the new trail, as an alternative to walking along the pista, to arrive at Wp.9 (see Walk 39 and map section). Now we are climbing the eastern valley wall to pass a ruined cottage on our left (Wp.4) at 4.4km and a 'Naturaleza' sign. Then it's back to easy strolling, or driving, to pass a forest track crossing the *pista*, 4.7km just before coming to a junction at 4.8km (Wp.5). 'Agua Agria' is signed up to the left as we continue front right on the main *pista* signed 'Barranco Río (sin salida)'.

We cross the municipal boundary 'TM Granadilla' at 5.1km to pass a *pista* off to our left, 5.3km (Wp.6) signed 'Agua Agria', the route of our 'masochist' option (C). A forest trail is passed at 5.6km just before a more major junction, 5.8km (Wp.7), where a cobbled donkey trail goes left and a barred *pista* runs off to our right. Past another chained *pista* off to the right, 6.1km, we reach the start of car parking along the side of the track and the path junction, 6.5km (Wp.8), for the 'official' start of the **Paisaje Lunar** walking route.

(B) Main Walk

At the start of the path (Wp.8 0M) a sign informs us that **Paisaje Lunar** is 45 minutes, **Valle de Ucanca** is 3 hours and **Degollada de Guajara** is 3 hours 45 minutes. We set off along the stone-lined trail through the pines to pass a second sign before coming to a cross-roads of paths (Wp.9 7M), with the new trail to **Vilaflor** signed left. In a couple of metres we keep left to follow the main path steadily uphill through the young pines. This easy woodland path meanders through the forest before climbing over a small hump, then running out into a lava field (Wp.10 13M). Over the lava, we climb through pines again to catch our first glimpses of the white pumice rock of **Paisaje Lunar** through the trees (Wp.11 25M).

A section of the lunar rockscape

A white arrow confirms our trail as we climb to the highest point of our route (Wp.12 1866m) before dropping into a valley to cross the water runoff (Wp.13), then passing a large pine to reach a *mirador* viewpoint overlooking the lunar landscape (Wp.14 36M), one of the best photo opportunities on the route.

The white and beige pumice rocks appear close, but there's still a little way to go. Our trail runs along the western wall of a steep valley, cistus bushes adding to the mature pines and *retama*, to cross the water runoff (Wp.15 43M). We pass another large pine before a path junction (Wp.16); the TS8 heads left up the black *picon* slope to **Montaña Arenas**, another path goes straight on, and the TS7 is arrowed down to the right. Going right, we descend carefully to cross a watercourse (Wp.17) to the edge of the surreal lunar rockscape (47M).

After taking a break under a large pine we continue down the narrow path (0M) carefully picking our way down to a watercourse and over to a path junction (Wp.18); the left hand path ascends through the lunar rockscape on a higher route to the junction at Wp.16.

Turning right, we pass another section of lunar rockscape before coming onto a woodland path running along the eastern side of this floriferous valley, cushion-like yellow lotus plants lining our route as if deliberately planted there. Our route swings left (Wp.19 10M) to bring us onto a bare ridge (Wp.20) studded with golden-needled young pines. Over a steel pipe, we cross a water runoff and come onto a second bare ridge. Heading down the ridge line, a white arrow on a rock (Wp.21 18M) confirms our route as we cross another steel pipe to come amongst pines, then climb up the eastern ridge to another white arrow (Wp.22 22M).

We follow the path down, crossing a steel pipe, as the sturdy chalets of **Campamento del Madre Agua** come into view across a large valley. Our path down the spur requires careful footwork, water erosion not helping as we swing left below a large pine to drop down and cross the water runoff (Wp.23 34M).

Then it's up onto a *pista* (Wp.24), 'Paisaje Lunar' signed back the way we've come. Now it's an easy stroll down the dirt road as it curves round to the campsite entrance, though our preferred route is to step off the road onto a trail (Wp.25) which leads down to a bare ridge studded with young pines and the first of the sturdy chalets. Down through the encampment, past the main tap and 'Gualivao' sign on a tree, we meet the *pista* again (Wp.26 41M).

Route finding is easy as we stroll down the broad track to a signed T-junction (Wp.27 45M) to turn right. After a short descent the *pista* runs through pines to cross a 'black sand' river (Wp.28 49M), passing a walking trail off to our left (Wp.29) as our track starts climbing. Our apologies for this rather uninspiring section, as we face a relentless uphill slope all the way along the *pista* to our starting point (Wp.8 68M).

(C) Pista Agua Agria
Mountain bikers, drivers of tough four wheel drives, and masochistic walkers can enjoy this long *pista* through the mountains above **Vilaflor**. Do not attempt this route in a normal car, or in bad weather. See map for the route which we consider one of the best off-road drives (in a Landrover) in Tenerife though sections can get washed away and unprotected vertiginous drops require full concentration.

From the junction on **Pista Madre Agua** (Wp.6) we swing up onto the narrow *pista* to come up to a cute bridge over a ravine (Wp.30) before climbing up to a T-junction (Wp.31) where we go right; going left

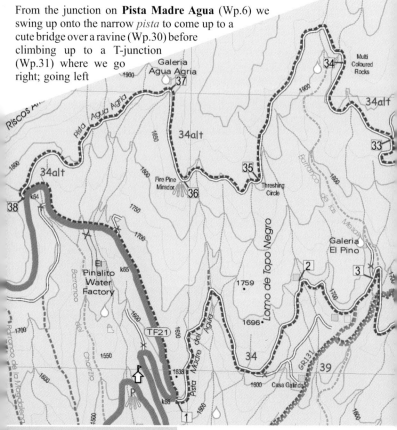

will take you back down to the **Pista Madre Agua** at Wp.5. Now it is up through the trees, passing a *pista* off left (Wp.32) plus a crude forest trail off right (Wp.33).

Now we come to the most difficult section as the track swings along the side of a very steep valley (unprotected vertiginous drops) to run through a region of unusually coloured rocks (Wp.34). Sections of the *pista* washed away in previous rains have been crudely rebuilt, requiring some skill to negotiate. Coming back amongst the forest, we pass a strangely located threshing circle (Wp.35) and eventually climb up the very rough *pista* to **Fire Pine Mirador** (Wp.36) where we can take a break accompanied by one of the south's most awesome of views.

After the *mirador* there is more rough track before we reach **Galería Agua Agria** 'sour water' (Wp.36) from where it's rough going, particularly on the descent down onto the TF-21 (Wp.38) just above the km.24 marker. If you've walked this route so far, then you have an easy 2km stroll down the TF-21, passing the entrance to the **Fuente Alta** water factory, to the entrance to **Pista Madre Agua**.

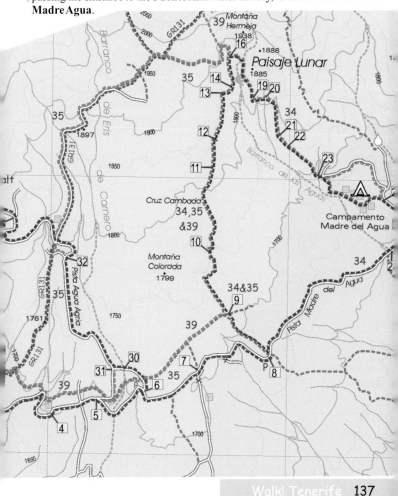

Paisaje Lunar is one of Tenerife's most popular high altitude walking routes. When we introduced 'Lunar Orbit 2' these landscapes were little known but this is changing rapidly with the new **GR131** (Wpts 14 to 25) and **Paisaje Lunar - Vilaflor** (see Walk39) trails having been created. These now provide an option to extend our original route by taking the **GR131** (at Wp.25) downhill until it meets the **Vilaflor** trail where we turn east to follow that new trail back to Wp.2.

Fit mountain hikers wishing to ascend to **Degollada de Ucanca** or **Degollada de Guajara (GR131)** should note the junctions at waypoints 14 & 15, which pinpoint the two trails in this previously little known region.

Access by car: see Walk 34, if the **Pista Madre del Agua** is closed the nearest parking is at **Big Pine Mirador** opposite the forest house above **Vilaflor**.

Our official starting point is reached by driving 6.5 kilometres along the *pista* **Madre del Agua** to the signboard for the **Paisaje Lunar** route (Wp.1 0M). Following the same outward route as for Walk 34, 'Paisaje Lunar', we pass a second signboard, then go right and left at the **Vilaflor** path junction (Wp.2 8M), following the 'Paisaje Lunar' signboard.

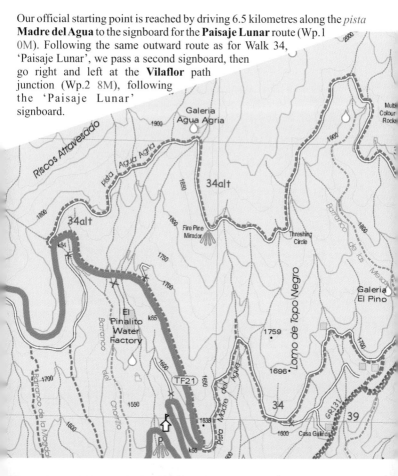

Our trail takes us steadily up through the woods and onto lava (Wp.3), then a mixture of lava and pine woods (Wps.4, 5, 6, 7 & 8) up to a *mirador* viewpoint overlooking the **Paisaje Lunar** rockscape (Wp. 9 40M). Our path runs alongside the steep *barranco* before crossing its watercourse and coming to the junction of paths (Wp.10 44M) below a black *picon* slope.

From the junction (0M), we trudge straight up the black *picon* ('TS8' & NW) to a stone marked with a green dot to go left off the black sand (Wp.11 3M) and into the trees where a steep black sand path climbs right alongside the *barranco*. That short example of an energy-sapping black sand ascent should warn you off old walking guides which use such routes in this region, as there are proper rock and dirt ascents to the **Degolladas Guajara** and **Ucanca** reached from later in our route.

We stay on the woodland path which contours around above the *barranco*. Here it's easy to miss our route off to the right (uphill, and Wp.12) as the main path leads straight on before petering out amongst the rocks. A steep climb brings us up onto the ridge line where our path swings up the ridge past a white arrow, to the western side of the ridge and across a *barranco* watercourse (Wp.13 21M). Now we climb steeply up another ridge before the gradient moderates and our path, heading west, changes to a *picon* base for us to come up to a junction (Wp.14 31M) with the **GR131** where going right (NE) would lead us onto a strenuous ascent to the **Degollada de Guajara**.

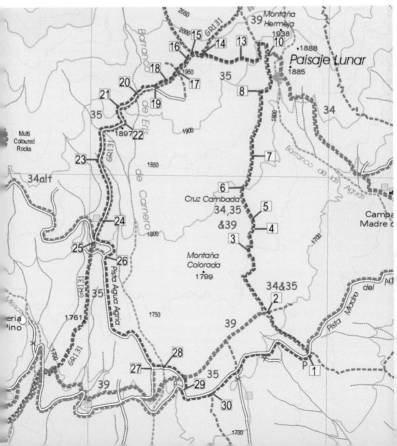

We go left to continue on the main **GR131** trail which runs gently downhill for us to come to a junction (Wp.15) where the **Valle de Ucanca** path goes right (NW). Originally this route was a faint path through the pines but becoming a section of the GR131 has produced a broad trail that passes an old water canal (Wp.16), with a sign to 'Pista Forestal Madre del Agua 1hr', as we head gently downhill through the pines (SW) to cross an old forest trail (Wp.17 34M).

Past a small cairn, we head towards a survey marker post (Wp.18), our trail now on a *picon* base. We come out of the pines into a lava rock landscape, our path running down a small defile before running out to join a little-used *pista forestal* (Wp.19 40M).

... a lava rock landscape ...

Turning right, we follow the rock road down to cross the smooth polished watercourse of the **Barranco de Eris de Carnero** (Wp.20) and continue downhill across a ridge, after which the *pista* is severely water eroded as it runs down past a rock 'cannonball' (Wp.21) on our left. Our route gets smoother and, just as it levels out, swings right (Wp.22) to drop into a valley where eroded pumice cliffs on our left face young green pines on our right. We cross a small watercourse and continue downhill, the *pista* becoming more eroded until we cross another water course (Wp.23).

Now it is easy strolling through the pine woods to pass a dilapidated cottage on our right (Wp.24) just before we drop down quite steeply on a very eroded section, to meet the **Pista Agua Agria** (Wp.25 65M). Going left on the pista we pass a track on our right (Wp.26) during our easy stroll down to a junction (Wp.27 86M). Keeping left on the main *pista* we drop down to cross a cute bridge spanning the **Barranco de Eris de Carnero** (Wp.28) and cross the **Vilaflor** trail before dropping down to meet the **Pista Madre del Agua** (Wp.29 90M); our alternative start and finish point. Turning left (SE) our *pista* passes a trail on our right (Wp.30), then a donkey trail left and a *pista* right before arriving back at our start point (103 minutes from **Paisaje Lunar**).

Alternative 'Scenic' Finishes
At Wp.25 continue straight ahead on the **GR131** until it meets the **Vilaflor** trail (see map) where we go left (SE) to follow this trail as it crosses the pista between Wps 28 & 29 before arriving back at Wp.2; or simply take the **Vilaflor** trail when it crosses the pista to return to Wp.2.
While we call these 'Scenic Finishes the views from our original pista route are actually better than from the **Vilaflor** trail's route through the pine woods.

Montaña Guajara dominates the sharp escarpment which encloses the southern wall of **Las Cañadas**. Viewed from the **Parador**, with sheer cliffs ringing its summit, it looks indomitable. In truth it's a straightforward, if very strenuous, ascent on our chosen route. We include the alternative descent/ascent as a warning, not just because it is difficult, complicated and potentially dangerous (it <u>is</u> all of these things), but because it used to be the most walked route.

You'll notice how thin the air is when you start the two ascent sections - not so noticeable is how much you sweat, so take three ½ litre bottles of water each and drink them en route. **Guajara**'s plateau summit can be cold and windy, so take a jacket no matter how good the weather looks. Do not be mislead by the walk descriptions appearing in some guide books, this is a tough route described by authors who have been there!

On arrival in **Las Cañadas** a 10-20 minute break (**Parador Café** if open) is recommended to enable you to acclimatise to the altitude.

** if opting for the alternative descent * at the **Parador Café**

Access by bus: N°342 from Las Americas & Los Cristianos, N°348 from Puerto de la Cruz; there is only one departure and return of these routes each day, so make sure you don't miss your bus! Alight at the **Parador**, then follow our Walk 30 'Toffee Mountain' route in reverse to our start point at the vehicle barrier on the **Siete Cañadas** *pista*.

Access by car: The park authorities have closed off access to the dirt *pistas* such as **Siete Cañadas** which used to provide a lot of car parking, thus putting increased pressure on the **Mirador Ruleta** car park and the small amount of road side parking near the **Parador Café**. After parking, follow our Walk 30 'Toffee Mountain' route in reverse to our start point at the vehicle barrier on the **Siete Cañadas** *pista*.

We start out from the vehicle barrier on the **Siete Cañadas** *pista* (Wp.1 0M) with an easy stroll curving around the honey-yellow **Piedras Amarillas** rocks in a gentle climb. As the *pista* comes up to take a climbing loop, we step off onto a faint trail (Wp.2 10M) for a steady zigzag climb up its shale surface, easier to ascend than descend, to rejoin the *pista* (Wp.3 14M). It's back to easy strolling now, looping into a valley with a huge tilted rock looming over us, **Montaña Guajara** high above us to the south. We stroll down past the **Sanatorio** dirt road (Wp.4 27M) and now looking for the **GR131** path on our right (Wp.5 32M).

Leaving the **Siete Cañadas** crowds behind, we follow the path (SE) in a steady climb with the yellow-lichened cliffs of **Guajara** above us on our right. It's a clear path but the thin air soon takes effect as we climb in lazy zigzags, pushing our way through Teide broom (Spartocytisus supranubius), also known locally as 'Retama del Teide', which threatens to take over our route in places. At lower altitudes this would be an easy ascent, but at over

On the Degollada de Guajara

2200 metres altitude it feels like a major climb as we toil relentlessly upwards. Our reward comes as we crest the ridge onto the **Degollada de Guajara** (Wp.6 68M) which provides us with magnificent views over **Las Cañadas** to the north and down the **Barranco del Río** to the south, plus some comfortable rocks to sit on while taking a break.

The path coming onto the *degollada* from our left, offers a strenuous ridge route from **El Portillo**; there's another path off to the right, while our route is straight over the pass.

Suitably refreshed, we set off from the **Degollada de Guajara** (0M) on the main **GR131** path (SW), descending past white rocks as the path curves around the huge bowl at the head of **Barranco del Río**. A short descent brings us under white pumice cliffs before our path starts climbing up through a tumble of rocks to a junction (Wp.7 8M) marked by a blue and white metal post. Ahead, the **GR131** running down a black *picon* ridge towards **Paisaje Lunar** is visible, while we turn right (W) to start the long ascent to the summit of **Montaña Guajara**. Small cairns assist wayfinding along the faint path as it takes to a small eroded gully (Wps.8 to 13 act as direction finders) for a breathless ascent in the ever thinner air.

A steady, relentless ascent (with plenty of breaks) brings us to the end of the gullies and onto a slippery white and mauve *picon* path lined with small cairns (Wp.14 32M) to pass a path off to our right (Wp.15 38M). It is onwards and upwards on our path until we come to overlook a sharp gully (Wp.16 53M). Here the 'official' path takes a precipitous drop into the gully so to avoid this potential accident we go right and up a small *picon* ridge to come onto stony ground where we curve left to rejoin the path (Wp.17 57M).

'Path' is perhaps too grand a word as it frequently disappears amongst the stones and Teide broom, but we keep heading upwards towards the ridge (NW), guided by cairns and waymarks to come onto the plateau summit (Wp.18 77M). After that thin air ascent, we recommend a relaxed stroll around the plateau taking in the different views.

At its centre is a large rock enclosure with a stone table and seats, the remains of an astronomical observatory and living quarters set up in 1856 by Charles Piazzi Smyth (brought up in Bedford, England) who spent three months completing studies and research in this clean, thin atmosphere, ideal for astronomers. Numerous grateful walkers now find the rock remains useful as windbreaks on this exposed plateau. While on the summit, you might look around for the trig point shown on military maps and pointedly mentioned in certain guidebooks - we've been all over this summit and cannot locate any Trig point!

Having enjoyed the views, it's time to descend. We strongly recommend that you return by the same route that we used to ascend, avoiding that precipitous gully. The paths are straightforward, with generally good grip, this time walking down the **Siete Cañadas** *pista* rather than the short cut path. About **120 minutes** will see you back at the vehicle barrier in good shape.

Alternative descent (but <u>not</u> recommended)
The route we describe here has everything you do <u>not</u> want in a descent; scrambling above vertiginous drops, difficult way finding (eased by PNF tracks and waypoints), slippery paths (where there are paths), crossing rock falls, intrusive Teide broom, slippery and slidey shale covered paths.

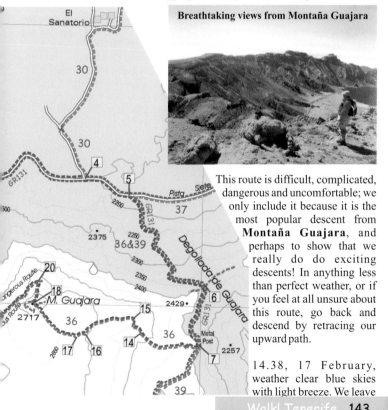

Breathtaking views from Montaña Guajara

This route is difficult, complicated, dangerous and uncomfortable; we only include it because it is the most popular descent from **Montaña Guajara**, and perhaps to show that we really do do exciting descents! In anything less than perfect weather, or if you feel at all unsure about this route, go back and descend by retracing our upward path.

14.38, 17 February, weather clear blue skies with light breeze. We leave the north-east corner of the rock shelter (Wp.19 0M) taking the clear path downhill (N) to awesome views down over **Las Cañadas** and to our toy car.

We pick our way down through a jumble of large cuboid rocks to a junction (Wp.20) where a short path runs out to a survey marker above vertiginous cliffs.

Back at the junction we go west, carefully looking for the cairns which mark the route, to come to a rockfall of large boulders requiring careful scrambling progress before we come onto a normal walking path, crossing a small scree field before our path runs below the cliffs and bulk of **Montaña Guajara**. We say 'normal path', but this is a slippery pumice *picon* descent, before coming to what we call a normal path (Wp.21 26M).

Next is a large rockfall (Wp.22 33M) which we climb through; by now you'll be getting an appreciation of the nature of this route! A 'nougat' style rock on our right (Wp.23) cheers us as we come into the sunshine as the cliffs have changed from brown to slate grey as we come under the cliffs again making steady and careful progress. We move out from the cliff wall (Wp.24 40M) to follow the path steeply down through rock detritus to negotiate a fall of giant scree followed by a slippery pumice *picon* slope to bring us to a rock ridge (Wp.25 57M). It seems a bit churlish to add that most of the scrambling and slippery sections take place above massive vertiginous drops down to **Las Cañadas**!

At the rock ridge we look out onto a very different tumbled landscape of mature Teide broom thriving on a steep rock-dotted hillside that runs down to the path junctions on **Degollada de Ucanca**. It's certainly less dangerous than the earlier section, as here it would be difficult to fall further than a couple of metres, but easier - no. In the tumbled rocks beneath the broom it's twist left, twist right, scramble down, and then repeat it all again and again and again. Various paths and cairns, have been pushed through the unforgiving vegetation. We follow what seems to be the main path (Wps.26, 27, 28 & 29) before arriving at a huge knob of rock (Wp.30 73M). A bit more twisting and shoving (Wp.31) and we come out into the open (Wp.32) to stroll (!) down onto the *degollada* (Wp.33) and over to the path junction (Wp.34 79M) where the path up the **Valle de Ucanca** joins us. Take a break, drink another ½ litre of water, and mentally prepare for the final descent.

From the *degollada* (0M) a clear path drops down and goes left (W) to a path junction (Wp.35). Our main path turns sharp right to descend on a tricky rock shale surface below a north facing cliff. Carefully picking our footsteps we move out from the cliffs onto the 'Thousand ZigZags' descent, passing a nice rock tower (Wp.36) on our left before coming down to a split in the trail with both routes cairned, before they come back together again. There are more twists and turns before our route straightens out to bring us onto a manicured yellow rock path (Wp.37); oh the luxury! At a large rock the luxury ends as we're back on a rough trail which brings us along to cross the water runoff beside the tarmac road (Wp.38 40M) and cross over onto the trail of Walk 30, 'Toffee Mountain', to cross the *malpais* to the **Parador** (49M).

We've always known about '**Siete Cañadas**' Tenerife's most popular high altitude walking route but it was some time before we decided to put this 'high altitude desert' experience into our Tenerife book. It's so easy to navigate that a description of the route could be; 'Start on the dirt road opposite **El Portillo Visitors' Centre**. Walk along dirt road until reaching a tarmac road and then turn right for the Parador' and there you have it!

Of course, there's much more to the route than that. Our research walk was carried out in the very worst conditions; summer heat wave with temperatures in the high thirties centigrade, into the face of a biting headwind that had closed the cable car service, and with a time limit of 4 hours if we were to catch the N°342 bus service at the Parador. 'Bumping Round Tenerife - Adventures on Titsa Buses' has the full story of our trek that day, plus hints on becoming 'Ghosts of the Mountain' by walking **Siete Cañadas** under the light of a full moon; now that is another memorable experience.

You must go prepared for the desert with full sun protection of hat, sunglasses, high factor sun cream, adequate clothing and footwear, plenty (2+ litres) of water plus snacks. Before tackling a four hour route at this altitude you should have experienced shorter routes such as Walks 30 to 33 to check your tolerance of walking at these altitudes.

* at the **Parador Café**

Access by bus: N°342 09.15 departure from **Playa de las Américas** to **El Portillo**, 16.00 return from the **Parador**. N°348 09.15 departure from **Puerto de la Cruz** to **El Portillo**, 16.00 return from the **Parador**. Note that the 348 allows 45 minutes more walking time, between arrival and departure times, if you choose to walk the route from West to East; which we recommend as the prevailing wind is behind you!

Access by car: Parking at **El Portillo Visitors' Centre**, some places near the **Parador**, and extensive parking opposite the **Parador**. Use the N°s 342/348 buses, or a rare passing taxi, to return to your start point.

It's 11.31 when we start off along the **Siete Cañadas** track (Wp.1 0M), strolling downhill and then up to where our Walk 31, 'Areñas Negras' trail leaves the track (Wp.2 8M); even this little section of downhill and uphill is rather enervating in the thin atmosphere. We've under four and a half hours to get to the **Parador** if we are to catch the N°342 back down the mountain; we'll have to walk at a fair lick with minimal stops. Once our GPS is reset from nautical miles to metric units, it shows that we are trudging through the broken hills at this end of **Las Cañadas** at around five kilometres an hour. Allowing for the stops to drink from our half-litre water bottles (we're carrying seven of these between us) and a couple of short recovery rests, we should just make it in time for the bus.

As we come out of the floriferous foothills into the crater proper (Wp.3 21M) the huge, endless vista unrolls before us, the **Siete Cañadas** track winding its way across the crater floor until it disappears as a pinpoint in the far distance. The vastness of what we have to cover is daunting to say the least - the landscape's sheer immensity takes your breath away.

After passing the **Areñas Negras** junction for our Walk 31 (Wp.4 28M), we really are on our own and although the GPS shows that we're keeping up our 5kmh walking speed, our progress across the vastness is imperceptible.

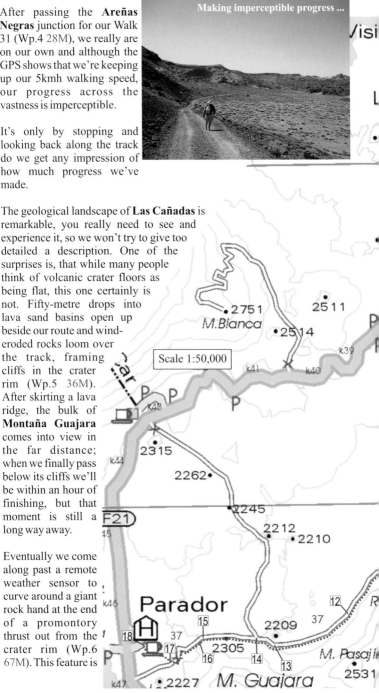

Making imperceptible progress ...

It's only by stopping and looking back along the track do we get any impression of how much progress we've made.

The geological landscape of **Las Cañadas** is remarkable, you really need to see and experience it, so we won't try to give too detailed a description. One of the surprises is, that while many people think of volcanic crater floors as being flat, this one certainly is not. Fifty-metre drops into lava sand basins open up beside our route and wind-eroded rocks loom over the track, framing cliffs in the crater rim (Wp.5 36M). After skirting a lava ridge, the bulk of **Montaña Guajara** comes into view in the far distance; when we finally pass below its cliffs we'll be within an hour of finishing, but that moment is still a long way away.

Eventually we come along past a remote weather sensor to curve around a giant rock hand at the end of a promontory thrust out from the crater rim (Wp.6 67M). This feature is

Scale 1:50,000

important not so much for its remarkable geology but for walkers' sanity, as without these markers this route could easily devolve into that nightmare scenario where no matter how hard you try you just can't make progress; the challenge of this route is both physical and psychological.

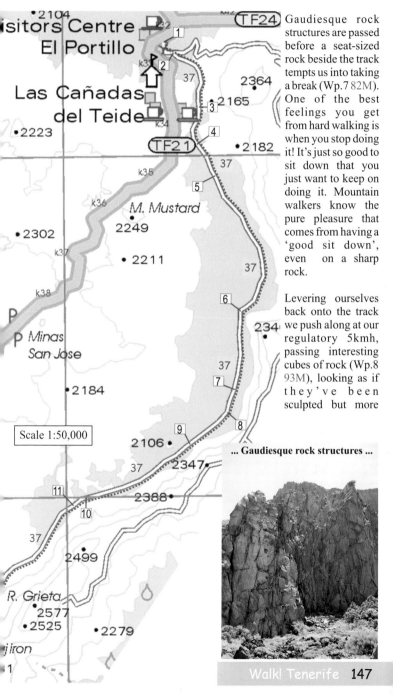

Gaudiesque rock structures are passed before a seat-sized rock beside the track tempts us into taking a break (Wp.7 82M). One of the best feelings you get from hard walking is when you stop doing it! It's just so good to sit down that you just want to keep on doing it. Mountain walkers know the pure pleasure that comes from having a 'good sit down', even on a sharp rock.

Levering ourselves back onto the track we push along at our regulatory 5kmh, passing interesting cubes of rock (Wp.8 93M), looking as if they've been sculpted but more

... Gaudiesque rock structures ...

likely to be unusual 'volcanic bombs' dropped here during the crater's formation.

Crossing with other walkers

We slog up a rise (Wp.9 105M) to pass a pre-shattered promontory thrust out from the rim, a scree of rock cubes showing the results of previous weathering. We crossed with walkers around here who were doing the route the other way round starting from the **Parador**, and are buoyed by the sight of **Guajara** coming back into view, much closer now but still a few kilometres away as we pass beneath an impressive peak in the crater rim (Wp.10 134M) above a pumice cliff.

Remains of huts at Wp.11

A steady downhill slope takes us past the remains of the shepherds' huts (Wp.11 139M), unused for over fifty years since grazing was banned in the crater, followed by an easy stretch of the track across a sea of lava grit; on the left is an amazing display of *tajinastes* at the foot of the

crater rim and higher up amongst the peaks.

This easy stretch runs out as the track swings up to cross a lava ridge in the steepest ascent yet. Down on the coast this would be a 'grinding' climb but up here in the thin air it's hard work.

The shattered hog's back rock after Wp.11

A shattered 'hog's back' rock beside the track, gives an excuse to stop for a photo, and then it's off again until we pass an interesting rock cone (Wp.12 180M) with an eroded rock wall alongside it where thankfully, the climbing ends.

We're keeping up to our 4-5kmh walking speed schedule as we sweep down towards the base of **Guajara** before another upward slope brings us to the junction with our Walk 36, 'Mighty Guajara' route (Wp.13 195M), where we take a couple of minutes break before tackling another slogging slope ahead to round an impressively shattered promontory.

We do manage a little spring in the step as we come along to the sanatorium track junction (Wp.14 201M) of our Walk 30, 'Toffee Mountain' route, the ghostly remains of the scattered buildings hidden from view. We sweep down between craggy shattered summits and the lava flow wall to come to a walking trail (Wp.15 214M) whose picky descent cuts off a long loop of the track. Back on the track (Wp.16 219M) we sweep down to a view over the **Parador**, below us is the dirt trail we will take across the *malpais* to the hotel.

If only there was a trail down the face of the lava flow that we're on the top of, we could save valuable minutes, but we must follow the long loop of the track down past a rangers' hut and vehicle barrier before reaching the trail's start (Wp.17 232M). The dirt trail twists and turns through the *malpais*, climbing gradually towards the **Parador**; we are going to finish before the N°342 departure time - we could even have time for a drink in the cafe, so we press on to reach the signboard (Wp.18) at the trail's end, exactly four hours after setting out from the **Visitors' Centre**.

We've arrived! We're in time for the N°342 return bus. We've survived all the depredations that **Las Cañadas** has thrown at us; long distance, high altitude, relentless sun, and that damn wind.

If you happened to be in the region of the **Parador** at 15.35 on Monday 3 July you might disbelieve that last statement, thinking that the two shapes near the signboard are actually giant boiled beetroots dressed as walkers that have then been covered in dust, grit and general dirt with the final added touch of caked on sweat; but no matter! We know we've survived one of our most foolish adventures ever as we hobble round to the café. Stepping into the mildly air-conditioned cafe we drop our packs on a table and I endeavour to buy some drinks while Ros makes for the *servicios*.

Buying drinks in the **Parador Café** used to be a tiresome experience when it was slow counter service, basically the pecking order was staff, bus drivers, friends and then anyone else if they could be bothered. Those days are gone now that its been remodelled to self-service, but there are no signs and I can't see any drinks. So I ask the guy on the till for 'two Fanta Limon please'; I'm too tired to speak Spanish. He points down the far end of the servery and says 'self-service', so I trek down the far end pick up two small cans of Schweppes Limon and return to the till. After paying the exorbitant four euros I ask for two glasses, again he points down the servery and says 'self-service', I hadn't noticed that the glasses are even further beyond the drinks. Eventually I have two cold drinks and two glasses on our table. It's a good job it's not busy in here because my experience is repeated again for the few customers that are gracing the café.

Really, I shouldn't moan too much because really we're grateful for any sort of café, even one as disorganised as this; though compared to the adjoining shop where it is difficult to find anything worth buying, it could be described as a masterpiece.

"That looks a bit of a challenge", we said while studying the old military maps and, "It doesn't appear in anybody else's guide book", as we discussed researching a walk from the **Parador** down to **Vilaflor**. Being familiar with the **Degollada de Ucana** on the crater rim and knowing of the *camino* down from **Las Lajas** to **Vilaflor**, all we had to do was link the two sections. Sounds simple? The plan was, bus to the **Parador** on the N°342, walk the crater rim possibly taking in **Roque Sombrero** before stopping for refreshments at **Las Lajas** followed by an easy descent to **Vilaflor** where we'd catch the last N°482 bus for **Los Cristianos**. That's 6½ hours if you are to catch the bus; we missed it by a margin but we were hampered by a broken walking sandal (Ros), shale covered downhill trails (our least favourite surface), and an attack of vertigo (David). If you're fit and quick you could make the 18.15 - even take in **Roque Sombrero** - though it's not for nothing that this route is 'The Big One' - it's a challenge route only to be undertaken in good weather.

5	6½ H	18 km	⛰	300m / 900m	⚠	⇄	🍴 2

Access by bus: N°342 09.15 departure from **Torviscas/Las Americas/Los Cristianos**. Return by N°482 last departure from **Vilaflor** at 18.15 for **Los Cristianos**.

Access by car: if you don't want to risk missing the 18.15 bus then you could drive to **Vilaflor** ahead of the N°342, park and bus to the **Parador**.

After the spectacular drive up to the **Parador**, we recommend you take a few minutes acclimatising to the thin atmosphere before setting off.

We start from the notice board on the southern side of the **Parador** (Wp.1 0M) on the narrow trail heading across the *malpais* to cross the metalled section of **Siete Cañadas** (Wp.2 11M) and head towards the crater rim. Our stone-littered path winds through the *malpais*, then starts climbing as we pass a waymark. A steady ascent in the thin air brings us past a second waymark, then at the

third waymark (Wp.3) our path clears of rubble and we come on to sand-coloured *picon*. Back onto a normal trail we are climbing steeply, taking breaks to enjoy the expanding views, to finally reach the top of our ascent (Wp.4 69M) and coming onto the rim just above the **Degollada de Ucanca**, a good place to take a break.

Heading steadily west

On maps there's a marked absence of height contours along the rim and as we set off along the path (0M W), we realise that on this broken landscape, we're probably the first map makers to walk this region. However, ther've been plenty of walkers before us leading to a confusion of paths in places, while other sections are refreshingly clear; no matter, the views are stupendous especially to the south. Alongside the path is a waymarked rock (Wp.5) as we head steadily west to encounter a scrambly ascent (Wp.6 8M) to pass through rock outcrops.

Our path brings us up onto the actual crater rim for more stupendous views, then becomes more difficult in a picky descent alongside dramatic drops to the **Ucanca** plain three hundred metres below. Our route turns away from the rim to negotiate the southern slopes of a rock outcrop (Wp.7 18M), then we're ascending again onto a broad *lomo* giving extensive views (Wp.8 32M).

... a tricky section of the path ...

We drop down to a saddle with a 'pn' sign, then up onto the crater rim to an area of great rock footballs (Wp.9 44M) which make convenient seats before tackling the next slope and a clambering ascent, guided by green dots, through large broken rocks (Wp.10 60M) to come under the cliff wall for another tricky section of the path. It's a wild mountain route, almost pathless below the cliffs, before climbing up through the rocks to a cairn (Wp.11 72M). Guided by a second cairn, we continue west, a path emerging as we ascend through Teide broom to pass a volcanic 'bomb' (Wp.12 76M).

Our route is confirmed by a green dot on a smaller bomb as we stroll through the broom in an 'upland plateau' landscape, stepping through an old wall and visiting the rim again before coming onto a miscellany of rocks. Green dots and cairns mark a route over the rocks heading towards a white dot and arrow in the middle distance. Passing the white arrow (Wp.13 85M) we come up to views down over tajinaste-dotted slopes to **Vilaflor** in the far distance. Past the white dot, we climb over a rock outcrop, then down and scrambling up again, this 'up and down' repeated as we follow white dot waymarking along the crater rim (Wp.14 100M) to edge towards **Roque Sombrero**. Finally we come onto a boulder outcrop (Wp.15 106M) with a white waymark fifty

metres ahead. Timings, realistic to this point, become a little surreal as David suffers a little vertigo moment. To reach the waymark involves lowering yourself onto a narrow rock shelf that overhangs the drop into the crater, edging across the shelf and then back up onto the rim. We look at it, then pick our way amongst the boulders looking for an easier way, which there isn't, so

we take a break to consider the matter. Beyond the boulder massif where we're seated we can see a clear path, and the thought of giving up and making the three-hour slog back to the **Parador** is marginally less appealing than dangling over a thousand-foot drop. Ros drops down onto the shelf and skips across to the white waymark, while David's traverse is somewhat slower before clearing the six-foot shelf (0M). Off the rock, we have the luxury of a path, then at a T-junction (Wp.16) a path literally drops into the crater as we go left on a steady descent through broom to come onto a clear path that climbs to reach a crest on the crater rim.

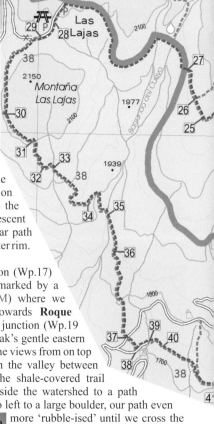

Now it's downhill to a path junction (Wp.17) shortly before a second junction marked by a large waymarked rock (Wp.18 9M) where we choose the downwards option towards **Roque Sombrero** and descend to another junction (Wp.19 13M) where a path heads up the peak's gentle eastern flank for those who wish to take in the views from on top of the 'Hat'. We head right, down the valley between **Roque Sombrero** and the rim, the shale-covered trail making for a picky descent alongside the watershed to a path junction (Wp.20 29M) where we go left to a large boulder, our path even

more 'rubble-ised' until we cross the watershed a second time (Wp.21 35M) and the path clears. Great rock buttresses punctuate the pine-clothed slopes which roll out into views over the south coast as we descend through the trees, unfortunately loose shale again covering the trail, so it's back to a slow picky descent on the serpentining path. Down below a large rock pillar we come to a path junction

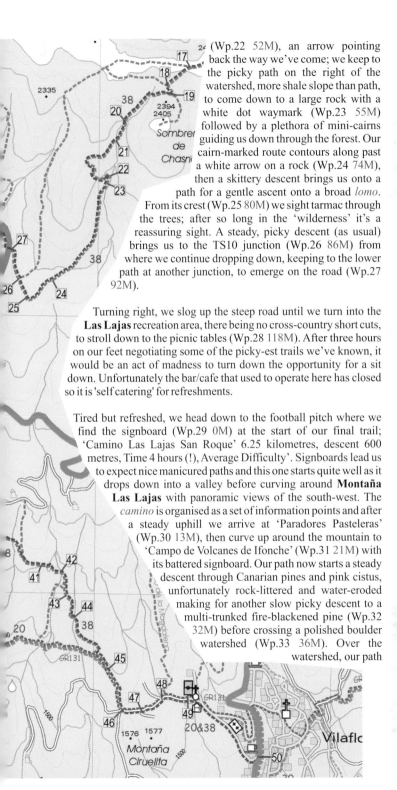

(Wp.22 52M), an arrow pointing back the way we've come; we keep to the picky path on the right of the watershed, more shale slope than path, to come down to a large rock with a white dot waymark (Wp.23 55M) followed by a plethora of mini-cairns guiding us down through the forest. Our cairn-marked route contours along past a white arrow on a rock (Wp.24 74M), then a skittery descent brings us onto a path for a gentle ascent onto a broad *lomo*. From its crest (Wp.25 80M) we sight tarmac through the trees; after so long in the 'wilderness' it's a reassuring sight. A steady, picky descent (as usual) brings us to the TS10 junction (Wp.26 86M) from where we continue dropping down, keeping to the lower path at another junction, to emerge on the road (Wp.27 92M).

Turning right, we slog up the steep road until we turn into the **Las Lajas** recreation area, there being no cross-country short cuts, to stroll down to the picnic tables (Wp.28 118M). After three hours on our feet negotiating some of the picky-est trails we've known, it would be an act of madness to turn down the opportunity for a sit down. Unfortunately the bar/cafe that used to operate here has closed so it is 'self catering' for refreshments.

Tired but refreshed, we head down to the football pitch where we find the signboard (Wp.29 0M) at the start of our final trail; 'Camino Las Lajas San Roque' 6.25 kilometres, descent 600 metres, Time 4 hours (!), Average Difficulty'. Signboards lead us to expect nice manicured paths and this one starts quite well as it drops down into a valley before curving around **Montaña Las Lajas** with panoramic views of the south-west. The *camino* is organised as a set of information points and after a steady uphill we arrive at 'Paradores Pasteleras' (Wp.30 13M), then curve up around the mountain to 'Campo de Volcanes de Ifonche' (Wp.31 21M) with its battered signboard. Our path now starts a steady descent through Canarian pines and pink cistus, unfortunately rock-littered and water-eroded making for another slow picky descent to a multi-trunked fire-blackened pine (Wp.32 32M) before crossing a polished boulder watershed (Wp.33 36M). Over the watershed, our path

Descending to the watercourse

is just as bad as we pick our way down to overlook a proper *barranco* (Wp.34 57M) into which we begin to drop. A massively rock-stepped section take us down to cross the watercourse (Wp.35 69M); on the left bank a proper path takes us zigzagging up before contouring along above the deepening ravine with impressive buttress walls, to 'Basaltos Antiguas' (Wp.36 78M); some of the oldest rocks in Tenerife. Crossing a watershed of the *barranco*, a short climb brings us into an open landscape of gentle rock slopes dotted with pines and cistus. After passing a walled pine we cross a dirt *pista* (Wp.37 92M), a picky path then bringing us back onto it (Wp.38 95M).

The *pista* becomes more water-eroded as we follow it downhill, passing above a water hut. A big green arrow directs us across a watershed (Wp.39 100M) to continue up a rough path which levels out and improves shortly before 'El Pinar' (Wp.40 105M), then reverts to its rough nature, at least with panoramic views of the south coast. We descend to cross a watershed before meeting concrete covered water pipes running alongside our route (Wp.41 114M) which provide comfortable seating.

Ros is wearing her toughest 'hard rock' walking sandals which chose this point to shed an ankle strap. A rough repair means our timings are even slower as we descend from a rock outcrop to cross a *barranco* watercourse (Wp.42 127M), more water pipes coming together in the valley, then coming to 'Eres' (Wp.43 130M) with its battered signboard. Green dot waymarks lead us across rough rocks, then we cross another watershed alongside steel water-pipes (Wp.44 136M). Green dots take us downhill to re-cross the water-pipe on the roughest of paths which becomes easier after we meet the GR131. We arrive at a water junction (Wp.45 147M) to catch a glimpse of our first house, which resolves itself into the pumping house of a roofed *embalse* as we descend the crude track to a crossroads of *pistas* set on a saddle (Wp.46 153M). Swinging left, we follow a green arrow (E) down a *pista* into a terraced valley of vines to pass two access tracks (Wps.47 & 48) before dropping down to civilisation in the form of the football ground and a tarmac road (Wp.49 161M).

After those rough trails the tarmac provides luxury strolling as we pass the impressive **Hotel de Lalba** to a junction where the main street swings left for an alternative finish in upper **Vilaflor**; we keep straight ahead on the minor lane which descends past the cemetery on our left and a home observatory on our right, the street dropping steeply as it becomes lined with houses, so steep that it would benefit from being staired. We skitter down through a sharp bend to drop onto the main road (Wp.50 171M), the street appropriately named **Calle la Ladera** - literally 'Ladder Street'! We're way past the last bus departure so we stumble up to the homely bars where we wash off the 'grime of passage' and recover with café con leche and 103 brandy while contemplating one unforgettably tough route. There's even time for a second round of drinks while the barman summons a taxi for our return.

Paisaje Lunar (the Lunar Landscape) is one of Tenerife's most sought after walking destinations for which we already offer two walking routes, Walks 34 (East) & 35 (West); these routes can be combined into a longer hike, so why another new **Paisaje Lunar** route?

Well, our routes are based on car access on the **Pista Madre del Agua**, which rather cuts out those bus-based walkers using Titsa's excellent services; quite a few walkers. Then the *pista* was closed for refurbishment and in 2007 we received reports of cars being ticketed for dangerous parking on the **Pista Madre del Agua** by rangers of the *Medio Ambiente*. Hire-car companies went ballistic; if you've seen the **Pista Madre del Agua** you'll understand how ridiculous these 'dangerous parking' fines are, though you could avoid the risk of being booked by parking at the camping area on Walk 34 (East) and getting the worst section of the route over first.

We knew that trails led down from the **Degollada de Ucanca** and **Degollada de Guajara,** this was before the **GR131** existed, so looking for a top range day-hike I roped in international travel writer Joe Cawley (author of 'More Ketchup Than Salsa') for a 'boy's adventure' day out. The full story of our day out in the mountains became a chapter in 'Bumping Round Tenerife' including the late N°342 bus, Joe's exploding boots and how we went mad in **Vilaflor**. I realised I had made a mistake in not taking the newly opened **Vilaflor** *sendero (*we took the *pista*), so to get the GPS records for my latest maps I walked the route again with modifications; hardly a hardship!. So much for my personal history on this route - let's get to the description.

This is a big day-out adventure at altitude; not quite as spectacular as 'Crater Rim Challenge' but also not as challenging. If you can handle the 300 metre ascent to the *degollada* (another 300 metres for the **Montaña Guajara** option) in the thin air (2,000+ metres altitude) you'll enjoy this long linear route giving a new view into **Paisaje Lunar** only seen by walkers using this route. Five walker rating is due to the altitude, ascents and distance.

* at start and end

Access by Bus: N°342 from **Playa de Las Américas** (09.15 via resort & **Los Cristianos**) to **Parador**, N°482 from **Vilaflor** petrol station 18.15.

Access by Car: car drivers could drive to **Vilaflor** and catch the N°342 from there.
On arriving at the **Parador** at 10.45, it's a good idea to take a 10 minute break to let your body aclimatise to the thin atmosphere at 2,000+ metres altitude, possibly running the surly gauntlet of the self-service café, or simply sitting on their outside terrace.
From the café terrace (Wp.1 0M) we stroll south across the access road turning circle to the notice board (Wp.2) where we step onto the narrow trail

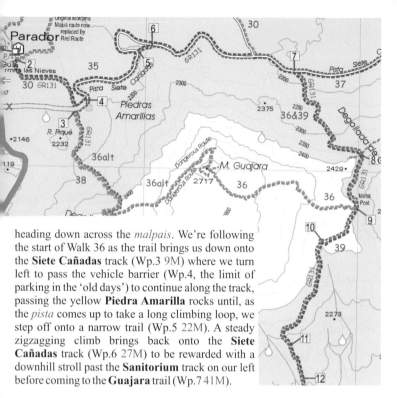

heading down across the *malpais*. We're following the start of Walk 36 as the trail brings us down onto the **Siete Cañadas** track (Wp.3 9M) where we turn left to pass the vehicle barrier (Wp.4, the limit of parking in the 'old days') to continue along the track, passing the yellow **Piedra Amarilla** rocks until, as the *pista* comes up to take a long climbing loop, we step off onto a narrow trail (Wp.5 22M). A steady zigzagging climb brings back onto the **Siete Cañadas** track (Wp.6 27M) to be rewarded with a downhill stroll past the **Sanitorium** track on our left before coming to the **Guajara** trail (Wp.7 41M).

The shortcut path (Wp.5)

A 300 metre climb would be fairly tough at sea level, here at 2,000+ metres altitude in the thin air it becomes a slogging ascent punctuated by frequent rests. Finally we're rewarded for our efforts by cresting the saddle onto **Degollada de Guajara** (Wp.8 77M) where I take a five minute break seated on the conveniently sized rocks before continuing. After that climb we have an easy stroll around the head of **Barranco del Rio** before our trail climbs up through a tumble of rocks to run along to a junction marked by a metal post (Wp.9 95M).

The trail to Degollada de Guajara (Wp.7)

If you are taking in **Montaña Guajara** today - recommended if you only have one day in this region and you have the energy - then go right, following the route of Walk 36 to the plateau-peak and back; my times are approximately 70 minutes up

and 50 minutes down plus sightseeing time but doubtless if you are considering this option you will be faster than me!

Taking your choice of the amazing views over southern Tenerife, we head off on the **Paisaje Lunar** path on a mixture of rock and dirt, the surface generally requiring concentration as we head SW. After turning into a small *barranco* to cross its watercourse (Wp.10) our route heads approximately south in a gentle downhill descent. We come down to an old, almost hollow, pine (Wp.11 125M) while ahead we have a magnificent vista of the black and gold *picon* sand slopes of **Montaña Las Arenas**, my favourite view on this route but down below us is the unexpected sight of a pristine stone lined track heading across the black *picon* sand of a broad ridge top plain to a junction in the distance.

A picky descent brings us onto the start of this unexpected track (Wp.12 133M) where at last we can stretch our legs at proper hiking speed to pass a faint trail off to our left (Wp.13) before coming to the junction (Wp.14, 145M).

The unexpected *picon* track (Wps. 12-14)

We must go right at this junction as going straight on, descending through the pines on an increasingly 'washed out' trail would finally deposit us at a *fuente*/aquifer east of the camping site, a long way from where we want to be.

We (that's me, Joe and hopefully yourselves) go right following a green arrow on the better-walked path lined by stumpy posts, through the pines on the edge of the ridge can be glimpsed the top of the unusual rock formations of **Paisaje Lunar** before we drop off the *picon* ridge into a rock and *picon barranco*. A narrow trail takes us down across the *barranco* watercourse to face a steep *picon* ascent. We slog up over the grit to the summit where our trail continues to a small *mirador* overlooking **Paisaje Lunar** (Wp.15 155M); this elevated *mirador* is by far the best viewpoint from which to take in the unique wind-sculpted white rock landscape.

A few metres off from the *mirador* we come to a path junction (Wp.16) where the sensible option is to continue straight ahead on a path descending through the pines, while on our left is a very steep *picon* scree heading directly for the famous rock landscape. Joe and myself step onto the forty-five degree scree, zigzagging down in a slalom descent curving round a rocky drop before running out amongst rocks (Wp.17) alongside the official path coming in from the south and the sensible route from our right.

If you go left you can explore the **Paisaje Lunar** landscape in close-up detail to your heart's content, but bear in mind the 18.15 bus departure from **Vilaflor** which is still a good hike ahead of us.

We head south (0M) on the official trail passing a *mirador* viewing point beside the trail (Wp.18) as we follow the clear trail down to a signed *sendero* junction (Wp.19 27M) above the *pista*; the junction 'PRTF 72' is signed 'Vilafor 4.5k' west along the new *sendero*. We're on a beautifully made *sendero* broad enough to walk comfortably abreast as we pass a path linking to the *pista* (Wp.20) with a sign 'Vilaflor 4.2k' confirming our direction. Our new route undulates through the forest to cross the **Agua Agria** pista (Wp.21) then the second **Agua Agria** access track (Wp.22).

Passing ruined cottages on our left, we meet the **Pista Madre del Agua** for a few metres before our *sendero* climbs into the woods again (Wp.23) to cross a ridge where we come to a junction (Wp.24) with 'Camino de Chasna', 'Paisaje Lunar 3.3k' (uphill), 'Vilaflor 2.7k'

The new *sendero* at Wp.23

The sign at Wp.24

(downhill), 'Paisaje Lunar 3.7k' (back the way we have come) signed on the waypost.

Going downhill, we drop steeply onto the **Pista Madre del Agua** at a stone-walled *sendero* entrance (Wp.25 60M), walls of a convenient height for us to take a seat

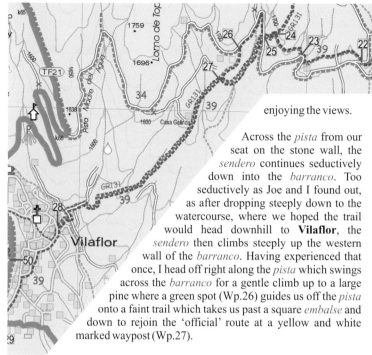

enjoying the views.

Across the *pista* from our seat on the stone wall, the *sendero* continues seductively down into the *barranco*. Too seductively as Joe and I found out, as after dropping steeply down to the watercourse, where we hoped the trail would head downhill to **Vilaflor**, the *sendero* then climbs steeply up the western wall of the *barranco*. Having experienced that once, I head off right along the *pista* which swings across the *barranco* for a gentle climb up to a large pine where a green spot (Wp.26) guides us off the *pista* onto a faint trail which takes us past a square *embalse* and down to rejoin the 'official' route at a yellow and white marked waypost (Wp.27).

The official route follows an old donkey trail down towards **Vilaflor** and while it is broad, it is also a very picky, knee-jarringly slow descent. **Vilaflor** is tantalisingly close as we pick our way down the trail to come onto a *pista* below the village. Across the watercourse of the *barranco*, a steep climb up the trail onto a paved driveway brings us to the first of the village houses (Wp.28).

Vilaflor at last

We go left down to a junction then right; keeping the bulk of the village on our right we choose streets heading south-west to come onto the village 'main street'. Strolling along this street which contours round below the main part of the village brings us out of the village to the 'petrol station' junction on the TF21 main road.

Our bus stop is at the petrol station (no sign); my choice is to seek refreshment at the bar/café (Wp.29 130M) on the opposite side of the TF21 while waiting for the N°482 bus arrival at 18.15.

Note that if you do not fancy the 'knee-jarring' donkey trail descent from Wp.27 you could continue on the **Pista Madre del Agua** from Wp.26 to the TF21 and then walk down the main road. This is much easier on your knees and has the added advantage of a choice of bar/cafes for refreshment.

40 ON TOP OF THE WORLD - MOUNT TEIDE

Mount Teide isn't a big mountain, it is a VERY BIG mountain; at 3,718 metres altitude, it's the highest point in Spain and you would need to travel thousands of kilometres to find anything this big. I make this point because many people/walkers have the impression that it is an easy walk; straightforward maybe but easy NO.

Teide is difficult for two reasons:-

- if you do not get a '*permisso*' from the ICONA office in Santa Cruz you will not be allowed to climb to the peak. Take the identification of everyone in your party (passports for visitors, DNI for residents) to the ICONA, Office Parque Nacional de Teide, Calle Emilio Calzadillo 5, 38002 **Santa Cruz de Tenerife**; third street left when heading east from Plaza de Espana. Only fifty people at a time per two hour time slot are allowed on the peak, so choose your two hour slot to suit your party assuming there are any vacancies on the day you plan to climb.

- thinner air means less oxygen for each lungful of air you breathe in, at these altitudes approximately 50% of the oxygen you get at sea level. Climbing 200 metres from the cable car to the peak is tough going requiring several rest stops, while the 1,400 metres ascent up the **Montaña Blanca** track and trail requires an extreme level of fitness.

If you <u>must</u> walk up **Teide** then this is one route where you would benefit from walking poles - well before the top you will be glad of your arms helping out your legs! Start out early, before dawn, on **Montaña Blanca** track to give yourself the most time for your climb; see Mike Reid's website www.fellwalker.co.uk/andalus.htm for his account of the ascent and descent.

We think the *teleférico* (cablecar) is a wonderful method of ascending 1,200 metres at these altitudes so this is how Joe and myself tackled the mountain on our 'Boy's Adventure' day out.

Access by Car (2 cars):- to avoid a long, and potentially dangerous road walk, from the end of the **Montaña Blanca** track to the *teleférico* station parking take two cars. Drive both cars out, to park one on the roadside near the **Montaña Blanca** track, park safely and considerately, then drive back to park your second car at the *teleférico* parking area.

Before setting off to the cablecar check that you have your ICONA 'permisso' and identification for each member of your party. This check plus queuing for your *teleférico* tickets (20 euros for visitors, 10 euros for residents, returns of course) and waiting for the car to arrive should give you ten minutes acclimatising to the altitude. The *teleférico* operators ensure the cars are packed to capacity making for an intimate ascent, the car usually stopping mid-way for a few minutes before continuing to its upper terminus. Once out of the terminus there is a viewing area, a good place for acclimatising to the higher altitude for another ten minutes while enjoying the views before setting off on our climb; there used to be a small bar here serving Lumumbas (hot chocolate with brandy) but sadly, it has been replaced with a toilet block.

When we feel adjusted to the altitude we set off from the cablecar station (Wp.1 0M) to walk to the 'ranger' junction where those without *permissos* are turned away towards the **Mirador de la Forteleza** trail. Two rangers check our *permiso* in detail against our identification (all your party must pass onto and out of the restricted peak en-bloc), before we're allowed to start climbing the well-made rock trail that leads up to the peak towering over us.

It's a busy trail even though limited to those with permits, so you'll get to meet plenty of other 'peak hikers' as parties leapfrog each other before taking rest stops, of which we take a number before reaching a *mirador* viewpoint turn in the trail (Wp.2). It's a well-made trail, a straightforward ascent except that at this altitude it's hard going with frequent rests before we reach the summit (Wp.3 40M). If you're thinking of a lonely mountain top you're in for a surprise.

Joe at the summit

Only fifty people are allowed on the summit in each two hour session but this means that all fifty are up here at once trying to bag a comfortable rock to sit on, or strolling around taking in the stupendous views of the other six Canary Islands, making for a crowded if convivial atmosphere.

You can never get enough of the views so it is with reluctance that we start the descent (0M) taking care on the steep trail as we drop down, passing hikers labouring up the path, to the ranger's control point (Wp.4 20M); where our *permiso* is checked against our ID again and returned to us. Now we are back amongst the general tourists as we take the trail out to the **Mirador de la Forteleza** to cross a small *barranco* before climbing up to the south facing **Mirador de la Rambleta** (Wp.5 23M). Continuing on the well-walked rock trail we pass the **Montaña Blanca** trail junction (Wp.6 32M), but rather than immediately getting into our descent we take the main trail out to the **Mirador de la Forteleza** large viewing platform (Wp.7 34M) to take in the northern views; spectacular. but after the views from the peak only a consolation for the 'non-permisso' general tourists.

After the 'Peak' and 'Tourist' *miradors* it's time to set out (0M) on the big descent so we backtrack to the **Montaña Blanca** trail (Wp.6) for our first stage of the descent to the **Refugio de Altavista**.

After the well made trails this is a rough, picky, narrow path requiring concentration on every step as we cross with the super-fit walkers on their ascent. A few minutes down we stand aside for the fluorescent orange shirts clothing three runners ascending the trail at pace; I kid you not, and Joe will confirm this amazing sighting. This surreal unsettling experience perhaps accounts for me taking a sliding fall, gashing my left wrist on the sharp rock, a couple of minutes later while the balance of my mind was disturbed!

Descending from the peak

View from the peak

We pick our way down to emerge on the small plateau dominated by the substantial, but closed up, **Refugio de**

Wp.8, the refuge at Altavista

Altavista (Wp.8 35M). There are comfortable rock walls to sit on so we take a break for a bit of lunch while enjoying the views across the crater to the opposite rim.

peak 3,718m

mirador

Montaña Blanca
trail 3,543m

mirador
ICONA Ranger Control

mirador

top of cable-car
3,556m

Refugio Altavista
3,280m

'Dragons'
eggs

join M.

Refreshed, we start out down the zigzagging trail (0M) from the refuge. We're winding down the face of the mountain before our trail runs out to an area of volcanic bombs (Wp.9 29M).

If you can imagine a high misty, snow-capped, lonely mountain with a dragon roaring round its summit then its only a small leap of the imagination to see these bombs as 'dragons eggs' though locally they are known as 'huevos de Teide' (Teide eggs). After photo opportunities we set off downward again to cross another region of Teide eggs (Wp.10 35M) before coming down to meet the **Montaña Blanca** track (Wp.11 54M); to this point there has been only one clear trail but now we have choices:- from the junction with its small rock shelter you could go right on the track, or front right on a trail over the *picon* to visit **Montaña Blanca** if you want to extend your route then returning back to

Below the refige

the junction for your final descent.

Joe and myself decide to continue straight on down the track, the good surface giving us the luxury of striding out for the first time today so we miss the first of the 'trail shortcuts' across the *picon* slopes that cut off loops of the track.

At a 'Teide Eggs' notice board (Wp.12 66M) we take to the trail shortcuts before rejoining the track for the final section. It's easy striding on the gentle descent, we're bowling along at about 7km per hour when the orange flashes of the runners pass us, soon to disappear into the distance. Just as we think we are dropping down to our finish point (we're seriously looking forward to the finish by now) our track has dropped into a valley for us to make a trudging ascent up around **Las Vueltas de Carnera** before the end comes in sight.

It's a stumbling finish as the track becomes seriously rough for the final descent in contrast to its pristine nature earlier, down onto the TF21 main (and only) road (Wp.13 109M) where we find the runners (members of Atletismo Tenerife) in voluble conversation; compared to our own moderate levels of mountain walking fitness the extreme fitness levels of these athletes on their altitude training has a slightly disturbing quality to it.

noticeboard

join M. Blanca track
2,730m

TF21 road
2,360m

Wp.9 with Teide Egg

At **Cruz del Carmen Centro de Visitantes** they helpfully provide a self-guided walk booklet for **Llano de los Loros**. Simplicity itself, the route shows aspects of forest life in the old days. What they don't tell you is that the route runs down the face of the forested escarpment, meaning a stiff uphill hike back to the parking area.

We extend the official walk onto the more impressive lower trail and add a little bit of easy tarmac to arrive at the **Las Mercedes Area Recreativa** picnic spot. It's an even stiffer hike back than the official route but well worth the effort to experience a classical section of the forest.

| 3 | 1½ H | 5 km | 150m / 150m | ↻ | 2* |

* at **Cruz del Carmen**

Access by car: Take the TF-121 north out of **La Laguna**, then the TF-12 to **Cruz del Carmen** where there is ample parking.

Access by bus: Titsa services Nºs 75 & 76 link **La Laguna** with **Cruz del Carmen**; check current timetables to confirm times and return services.

From the car park signboard (Wp.1 0M) we stroll down the broad trail into the forest to pass the example of the craft of 'cut tree heather' (Wp.2) before coming to a wooden barrier (Wp.3) where we follow the main trail down to the right.

At the '3' marker post

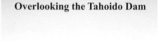

Overlooking the Tahoido Dam

The next official interest point is signed '5 Fertile Pocket' (Wp.4) followed by '3 Canal', our route now noticeably steeper, running down between earth banks to a signed junction (Wp.5) where we go over to the **Llano de los Loros** viewpoint overlooking the **Tahoido** dam (Wp.6 15M 881m), a picturesque end to the official route.

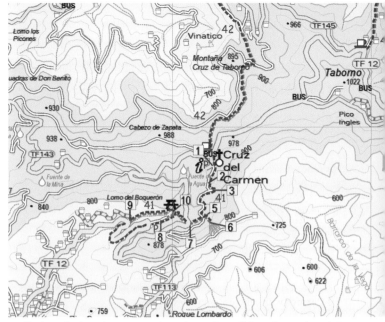

Back at the junction, we continue down the trail into deeper laurel forest to emerge onto the TF-114 road (Wp.7 22M). Across the road, our trail plunges into the old forest alongside a sharp cleft, rock steps assisting our steep descent down the old 'donkey motorway' of pre-tarmac days.

We drop down past a 'hitching rail' vehicle barrier to reach the **Las Mercedes** parking area (Wp.8 30M 840m). Instead of entering the recreation area, we continue down the TF-114 road facing the traffic, until we come to a signed trail which takes us back into the forest (Wp.9 44M). Our broad trail climbs through the trees and crosses the watercourse on substantial wooden footbridges before a final steep, tree-root stepped, climb brings us to the **Las Mercedes Area Recreativa** again (Wp.10 52M). How much more satisfying to take a break at the picnic tables after a bit of climbing!

One of the substantial footbridges

Our return from the 'hitching rail' (0M) is a slogging ascent back up the donkey motorway, across the TF-114 (Wp.7 8M), then up to rejoin the strollers on the official route (Wp.5 12M) to finally emerge back at our start point in **Cruz del Carmen** car park (Wp.1 28M).

We rather like **Cruz del Carmen** with its *mirador*, Tourist Office, large car park, market for local produce, bus stop and lively bar (though not so lively that they provide anything to sit on, apparently a local custom in the **Anaga**!). Here, at the gateway to the **Anaga**, the old donkey trail 'main road' crosses with modern tarmac, appropriately marked by an *ermita*. Several trails converge at this crossroads; today we follow the main trading route between the **Anaga** settlements and **La Laguna**, plus a few scenic diversions.

4	4H	10.8 km	460m / 460m	↻	2

Short Version	**Extensions**
Drive to **Las Carboneras** and complete the **Chinamada** circuit.	From **Chinamada** take the signed *sendero* to **Punta del Hildalgo**.
Access by car and bus: See the notes at the start of Walk 41.	From **Las Carboneras** take the signed *sendero* to **Taborno** (Walk 44) to link with Walk 43.

Each side of **Bar/Restaurante Cruz del Carmen** are *sendero* boards. We choose the eastern 'Las Carboneras 45m, Chinamada 1h 30m, Taborno 1h 30m' trail (Wp.1 0M). Immediately we're in the laurel forest on a broad woodland path which zigzags down with log-stepped sections (poor to nil GPS reception for most of the forest section of our route).

As the trail levels out we pass a path off to our left (Wp.2 8M), our route curving round a large, steep wooded bowl in the *cumbre* to pass a second path (Wp.3). After a small ascent we resume our inexorable descent through the trees. As we cross a ridge between two bowls (Wp.4 15M) a walking trail goes straight ahead, while we go down a log-stepped descent into the second bowl. As we catch glimpses of a dirt *pista* below us (Wp.5), a faint path goes off the main track, then we drop onto the *pista* past a 'hitching rail' barring vehicle traffic (19M).

The steep trail

Across the *pista* a 'Carboneras, Chinamada, Taborno' sign points us down a steep trail, dropping down through tight zigzags into a sharp cleft and past a waterpoint, just before crossing the cleft's watershed. Across the boggy watershed (26M), we head steeply up in a slogging ascent, the gradient easing before we emerge from the forest onto a dirt track to the surprising sight of brightly painted houses above us (Wp.6 28M).

Turning left, we head down the track and past a cottage with a quiet dog - unusual enough in this region to comment on - as we head towards a *casita* and electricity pylon set on the next ridge. Ignoring tracks into the fields we keep heading downhill, our track narrowing to a trail (Wp.7), ignoring a small path running straight ahead as we start climbing steeply up and right to the electricity pylon and the tarmac road (Wp.8 42M). Taking to the tarmac, we stroll down past houses and plots until we find the 'Chinamada, Carboneras' trail signed off the road on a right bend (Wp.9 48M). Down the manicured steps, we head down the trail beneath a rock/earth cliff with views opening up over a ribbon of tarmac road way below us and across to **Roque Taborno** in the distance. It's steeply down to a signed 'Chinamada, Carbonera' junction (Wp.10 52M) where we continue ahead on the **Chinamada** path.

Exceptional views from Wp.12

Contouring along beside a very steep ridge, we enjoy exceptional views before dropping down into the forest to a junction (Wp.11) where we keep right to climb back to our contouring altitude. We reach an abandoned *casita* sited above caves cut in the golden volcanic rock (Wp.12 67M), an idyllic picnic setting if you're taking a break.

From the *casita* our path contours round a steep wooded bowl before dropping to pass long-abandoned terraces, then we climb to excellent views on a corner (Wp.13 74M). Again, our route contours across the steep slopes, passing abandoned terraces before topping a crest (Wp.14 722m) and finding sections of the original boulder-laid *camino real*. Our route crosses to the eastern side of the ridge, a minor path going off to our right and **Chinamada** coming into sight as we descend steadily to a *mirador* viewpoint (Wp.15 90M). Dropping from the *mirador*, our path runs down past a cave with carved seat, to come onto a driveway at the first house and onto the road from **Carboneras** (Wp.16 96M) below cave house N°3.

We stroll down below more cave houses built into a promontory to the gaudily painted village square and go right to **Bar La Cuerva** (Wp.17) built into the rock (closed Mon & Tues). A short diversion following the 'Mirador de Aguade 15 mins' sign to overlook the massive rock eruption out of the *barranco* floor is recommended; in reality, it's a mere 5 minutes each way. From behind the village square the path to **Punta del Hidalgo** is signed down into the *barranco* for a linear route option.

From **Chinamada** (0M) we follow the tarmac lane to **Carboneras** - such an easy stroll down but such a slog uphill - noting the pedestrian way up to the promontory cave houses which provides an interesting alternative route to rejoin the road above Wp.16. Tarmac strolling is normally relaxing, but as this is all on a relentless incline, the opportunity of a lane-side picnic area (Wp.18 12M) is too good to miss; then we continue slogging uphill to a *mirador* (20M), taking a few seconds to admire the spectacular views into **Barranco de Taborno** and across to **Roque Taborno**. The lane's gradient eases to a stroll before dipping downhill, then a steep slogging ascent takes us into **Carboneras**, panting gratefully up to the doors of **Bar/Restaurante Tesegre** (Wp.19 37M), just below the village square and bus stop.

The final loop in our adventure should be easy as we set off from the bus stop (0M) to stroll down past **Bar/Restaurante Valentin** opposite the signed turning for **Taborno** (Wp.20) and leave the settlement behind. Just as we're thinking we must have missed the path back to Wp.12, we find the unsigned stairway (Wp.21 6M) climbing up from the road. 'Las Laderas' is well named, if unsigned, as we have a ladder/staired ascent until the gradient eases to merely steep.

On the climb after Wp.21

We slog up through bracken and tree heather, our ascent relenting as we round the spur and the pylon at Wp.10 comes into sight. A *fuente* provides a welcome break in the ascent (Wp.22 22M 727m), before we climb back up to the path junction at Wp.10.

You'll well remember the outward route in reverse; a steep ascent to the road, gruelling tarmac uphill before turning off on our outward path, easy up to the outlying *casita* then slog up to the houses and dive back into the forest, zigzagging up to the *pista* then past the 'hitching rail' to climb up through the forest in an almost never ending ascent to emerge alongside the bar at **Cruz del Carmen** (83M). The laurel forest saves us from the sun but it's still a gruelling three hundred metre ascent in any language, the bar's ice cold Dorada tasting like nectar - but what wouldn't we pay for a bar stool to perch on!

The **Ruta Littoral** along the **Anaga**'s spine makes a good jumping off point for adventures in this dramatic landscape, just remember that every step down has to be matched by a step back up! Modern tarmac roads to **Taborno** and **Las Carboneras** are dramatic enough but the old *camino real* trails of the donkey power days are far more breathtaking, particularly on the uphill return. We pull no punches, this is one of the great spinal routes, dramatic in descent as well as ascent.

4   2½ H   6 km   390m   390m   1*

*When we originally walked this route (March) there were two bars in **Taborno** including the **Nightmare Bar** but both had closed by July!

Access by car: some parking places near **Casa Carlos**; be sure not to block any access. Some on road car spaces before entering **Taborno** but take care not to block the bus-turning circle.

* at **Casa Carlos**

Extensions
Circuit of **Roque Taborno**; 5 walker, add 60 minutes. Descent to **Afur** and back up the *camino rural* to **Taborno**; 5 walker, add 90 minutes.

Access by bus: Bus N°75 links **La Laguna** to **Taborno**, or take the N°76 and N°77 from **La Laguna** to **Casa Carlos** and walk the route in reverse.

We start out from **Casa Carlos** (Wp.1 0M) on the tarmac lane beside the building signed 'Taborno 40m, Afur 1h, Taganana 2h 30m' heading gently downhill as tarmac becomes concrete, then strips by house N°64, before narrowing to a trail and plunging into the forest (Wp.2 4M). Straight down a narrow spur, we head unswervingly for **Taborno** (N), whose sheer sides could be considered forested cliffs rather than slopes in many places; our well-made, broad trail was the donkey main road up from **Taborno** in pre-tarmac days. Passing a path down to our right (Wp.3) we come to house N°66 set below the trail (Wp.4); no vehicle access but with mains electricity.

After picking our way down the steep and sometimes slippery, trail, we are greeted by a drawbridge-like dirt path a metre wide, across the flat top of a very steep-sided earth bank (17M) that links us to the next rocky promontory; it's so neat, you'd think it was man-made rather than being a natural feature. After a second dirt 'drawbridge' our trail reverts to its original nature as laurel is replaced by tree heather and eucalyptus alongside the route. Passing an earth cave with seat, (Wp.5), we come down to views across to **Carboneras** (Wp.6) and at a hairpin bend **Roque Taborno** comes into sight ahead (27M).

The **Taborno** road is a narrow ribbon far below as we head relentlessly down the ridge, zigzagging through tree heather to a natural *mirador* (Wp.7 34M) with spectacular views over the **Barranco de Afur**. We cross another 'drawbridge' for an unusual slight upward incline, followed by a rock-stair ascent to the **Afur** junction (Wp.8 38M) where the descent to the settlement drops steeply down to our right. Our broad dirt trail curves around the mountainside above steep drops to the little road way below to yet another 'drawbridge' before descending again, now with ridge-top views. A slight ascent to a fenced water tank, then a steep, sometimes stepped, descent

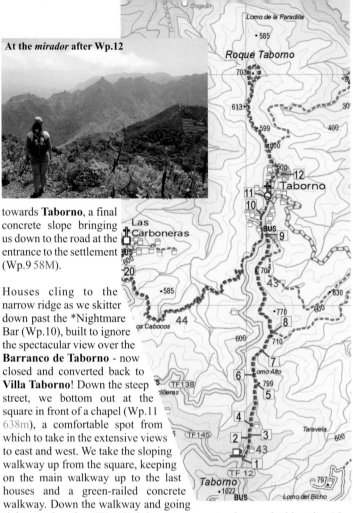

At the *mirador* after Wp.12

towards **Taborno**, a final concrete slope bringing us down to the road at the entrance to the settlement (Wp.9 58M).

Houses cling to the narrow ridge as we skitter down past the *Nightmare Bar (Wp.10), built to ignore the spectacular view over the **Barranco de Taborno** - now closed and converted back to **Villa Taborno**! Down the steep street, we bottom out at the square in front of a chapel (Wp.11 638m), a comfortable spot from which to take in the extensive views to east and west. We take the sloping walkway up from the square, keeping on the main walkway up to the last houses and a green-railed concrete walkway. Down the walkway and going right at a junction (Wp.12) brings us to a *mirador* overlooking the **Afur** valley; a little-known vista not to be missed. Going left from the junction, we drop down through trees to pass below a house and then out into the open to stroll out to a path junction (Wp.13 75M). Continuing to follow the main path, we climb up past a fenced cave-cottage onto the headland for the best view of **Roque Taborno**.

Extension

From the headland, a path runs out to encircle the massive rock, an exposed path requiring a good head for heights which should only be tackled in calm conditions; for some reason it always blows a gale when we are here.

Having done the descent into **Taborno**, you know what to expect on our return. We're not the fittest of walkers, so were pleasantly surprised to find ourselves at the **Afur** junction in 21 minutes and at the earth cave in 42 minutes for a longer break than the many others en-route, and alongside **Casa Carlos** at 68 minutes; times taken from the start of the trail by the 'Taborno' sign.

This short route between two of the **Anaga**'s ridgetop villages is useful for linking Walks 42 & 43. We follow an old donkey trail dropping into and climbing out of the **Barranco de Taborno**. Sections of the route are frequently overgrown so secateurs are recommended. Although short, it is quite energetic. For readers requiring a gentler tour, we recommend following the tarmac road around the bowl of the valley; this is simple with no major gradients, will not be slippery in wet weather, and has rustic log crash barriers which make quite comfortable seats should you want to take a break (just don't lean back too far) and it will give you a view of the **Anaga** but not the 'up close and personal' extreme view that our hiking route provides.

*In **Las Carboneras** you have a choice of **Bar/Restaurantes Tesegre** and **Valentin**.

Access by bus: N°75 service from **La Laguna** departs 09.15*, 13.05, 15.15, 18.45. Return 10.00*, 14.00, 16.15, 19.45. * does not call at **Las Carboneras**.

Access by car: If you walk this route 'out and return', we suggest you park on the roadside before **Taborno** and walk to **Las Carboneras** for refreshments at **Bar/Restaurante Tesegre** before returning.

Dropping into the valley

Arriving in **Las Carboneras** by bus (Wp.1 0M) you have the option of walking up past the chapel to **Bar/Restaurante Tesegre** for refreshments before starting out. From the bus stop we stroll back down the road to take the narrow tarmac lane signed 'T a b o r n o 45M', opposite **Bar/Restaurante Valentin** (Wp.2 3M). Our lane drops down into the valley, then where the lane swings left towards a fenced enclosure, a substantial wooden 'Taborno' sign directs us down onto a small path. We drop down

onto the narrow walking trail running between the lane's support wall and vegetable plots before a rock stepped descent, needing careful footwork, takes us down past more plots in a side valley of the main *barranco*. Vegetation

Views back to Las Carboneras en route

pushes in on our path (secateurs useful) then surprisingly climbs gently up past white rock and widening to a comfortable walking width as it cuts across the steep wooded slopes to a junction (Wp.3 11M). We go down left to examine a plot of potatoes before correcting our mistake by climbing back up to the main path to continue straight ahead.

Passing a *teleférico*, its wire stretching up to the edge of the road high above us, we curve around the *barranco* wall to an electricity pylon (Wp.4) marking our transit into another pocket in its wall. A picky descent on rock steps takes us around a ruined hut camouflaged by vegetation, before continuing down through zigzags, vigorous plant-life enveloping the path - careful footwork needed. We come to a potato and pumpkin patch and pass below a green hut (Wp.5 22M). There's only one path across the *barranco* and as this is the last vegetable plot, our route is likely to be less walked and consequently more overgrown from this point. Another rock zigzag descent takes us across a watercourse, then our path pushes through a briar and bracken section before we enter, with some relief, into a section of tree heather.

For once our optimism is rewarded as our path winds amongst the steep forested slopes with just one more briar and bracken section before emerging into the open (Wp.6 32M) to see **Taborno** above us across the ravine. A steady to steep descent drops us down to follow the watercourse which our path then crosses (Wp.7 481m/1578ft). It's an easy guess that we're in for some serious climbing as our path heads steeply up the slope. Thankfully the trail is in good condition as we continue onwards and upwards with frequent 'get your breath back' stops. Finally we reach a path junction (Wp.8 57M) and keep left to walk alongside a briar-draped stone wall above a potato plot. Coming into the open, we climb up to an electricity pylon, just above which, at a turn in the path, is a tiny shrine to 'Señora Dona Effizez Carlos (1934)'set in a stone wall. A final slogging ascent brings us to emerge gratefully onto the **Taborno** road (Wp.9 66M). After that tough climb the gently sloping tarmac feels like luxury as we pass a 'Carboneras' sign to the bus stop at the end of **Taborno** village (Wp.10 72M); our Walk 40 ridge line route from **Casa Carlos** also joins the road at this point.

Views north-east from Taborno square

A simple stroll takes us past the 'Ventario Illario' signed path to the luxury of wooden benches on the village square below the chapel (Wp.11 75M). **Ventario Illario** is a tiny *tipico* perched on the ridge-top above the village, worth a try if it's open.

A ridge-top route with plenty of surprises and a delightful descent into the 'end-of-the-road' village of **Chamorga**. Spectacular *miradors* combine with woodland and spectacular flora to produce a true classic in every sense of the word. Paths are generally narrow requiring sure-footedness but are not vertiginous, at least in our experience.

Access by bus: Unusually for us this is a linear route designed to take advantage of the Nº247 Titsa service leaving **Chamorga** at 16.30 and 19.30, so time your arrival accordingly.

Access by car: Park in the **Ensillada Area Recreativa** area car park on the north side of the TF-123, 4.7km from **El Bailadero**; the recreation area picnic and barbecue area is laid out amongst the trees to the south of the road.

Short Walks
(a) To the peak of **Chinobre** and return.
(b) To **Cabezo do Tejo** and then return by strolling along the broad *pista*, barred to traffic, back to the TF-123 and then 1.5km of road walking (W) back to the parking area.

Starting from the parking area (Wp.1 0M) we follow a dirt track into the forest (NE) parallel to the road. Immediately we plunge into the dank forest (poor GPS reception). We stroll uphill, our track narrowing to a trail (Wp.2), becoming stone-stepped on the steeper sections. Ageless trees and lichen give the forest a fairy tale air as we curve up (N) to a junction (Wp.3 17M). Going left on the minor path we continue ascending (W) through the trees, glimpses of vast drops through the tree heather on our right revealing that we're climbing along the edge of cliffs.

The view from Chinobre

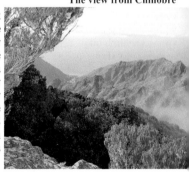

A final climb and clamber on rock bring us onto the summit of **Chinobre** (Wp.4 20M 924m); a broad rocky knob with trig point, poking above the trees like a geological periscope. On a bad day (cloudy) the views are simply spectacular, while on clear days they can unman even the most resolute poet. Remembering to pick up the GPS off the trig point, we return to the main path (Wp.3 0M) to continue towards **Cabezo do Tejo**.

We have an easy stroll down through the forest on the well-defined path, earth/mud stepped sections requiring careful footwork, to a junction (3M) where 'Chamorga' is signed down the path on our right and 'Bailadero' is signed back the way we've come; the signs old, rusty and decrepit, and possibly not long for this junction. Our route continues ahead as a pleasant woodland path running alongside the eastern edge of a ridge, generally downhill with steeper earth/mud stepped sections, (Wp.6 12M) but climbing a small crest before dropping again to negotiate a fallen tree (Wp.7), then

The great rock of Anambra

passing an impressive rock perched on the lip of the ridge (Wp.8 16M).

It's pleasant strolling until a stepped ascent takes us to another crest, then our woodland path crosses to the western side of the ridge (Wp..9) with impressive views and drops, glimpsed through the trees on our left. We're brought up short on this pleasant descent of the wooded ridge as, with a great gasp, we emerge from the trees to come nose to nose with the great thrusting rock of **Anambra** (Wp.10 32M) - a greater contrast between cosy woodland and this sheer pinnacle of rock rocketing skyward, would be difficult to find.

When normality returns, we follow the path around **Anambra** to plunge down into the forest once more. Now it is seriously down the slippery stepped woodland path with a final hairpin descent onto the broad pista (closed to traffic, 48M), that serves the **Cabezo del Tejo** *mirador* (Wp.11, total time 72M). Superb views over the northern coastline, exceptional except when compared with **Chinobre**, together with stone wall seating, makes for a natural break in our adventure.

From the northern end of the *mirador* (0M) our path drops (literally) steeply down into the forest on the worst mud-slide steps of the whole route before passing a natural rock *mirador* (Wp.12) where we come onto a proper walking surface. There's only one path and only one way; down through the steep wooded slopes until, after passing a faint path off to our left (Wp.13 11M), we come down to a

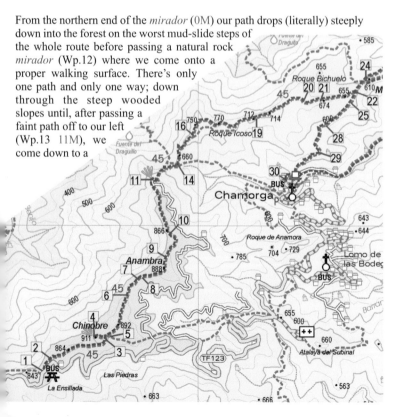

signed crossroads of paths on a saddle (Wp.14 16M). 'El Draguillo' (N), 'Tefada' ahead and 'Chamorga' (SE); a 25 minute shortcut to the village dropping steeply to our right. Across the crossroads, we climb steadily and then steeply on the woodland path to pass a natural rock *mirador* (Wp.15 24M), then a more vertiginous dirt *mirador* before finally slogging up to a crest (Wp.16 33M). Over the crest, the narrow woodland path circles a bowl, requiring surefootedness above the unprotected drops. We pass below spurs of rock (Wp.17) and get glimpses of **Chamorga** before arriving at a spectacular *mirador* (Wp.18 45M) set at the top of cliffs overlooking the **Roques de Anaga**; we'd advise you not to put any trust in the wooden railings.

From the *mirador* it is steeply uphill through stunted forest to a path junction (Wp.19 50M) to yet another *mirador*, followed by a rock outcrop (Wp.20 60M), making a break from the woodland. Finally we leave the woods behind (Wp.21) to walk above heather-covered slopes with views over the **Barranco de Roque Bermejo**. Endemic flora competes for star billing alongside our path as we come down to a junction (Wp.22), our final route to **Chamorga** going back right, before coming down onto the saddle at another path junction (Wp.23) by the **Tafada** ruined cottage (Wp.24 67M). From the saddle we have options to go north to **Las Palmas**, though this path was blocked by a landslide on our last visit, or on past the **Tafada** cottage to overlook the **Faro de Anaga**; you could descend past the *faro* to **Casas Blancas** and then return to **Chamorga** on the path up the **Barranco de Roque Bermejo**.

After a break in these beautiful surroundings we backtrack to the junction (Wp.22 0M) to take the **Chamorga** path; quite one of the most delightful paths in the **Anaga** though requiring surefootedness on its narrow sections and clambering descents, initially onto a well trodden path (Wp.25).

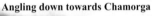

Angling down towards Chamorga

We angle down towards **Chamorga** across the flora-stuffed slopes to a set of handrails (Wp.26 11M) above a 'rock-stair'descent before the easy path resumes. Our next feature is a geologically interesting rock-stepped descent alongside a sloping cliff face (Wp.27) to come onto the luxury of a metre-wide comfortable dirt path (17M), taking us past the first terraces (Wp.28) before coming up onto a spur (Wp.29 26M) below a massive 'Devil's Head' rock while the spur is tipped by an oversize 'Friar's Rock'.

Our final descent is straightforward to come down and curve above the first houses (and bar!) of the settlement before dropping down to the tarmac road (Wp.30 41M); technically **Punta de Anaga** rather than **Chamorga** - but **Bar Chamorga** a few metres to our left is of more practical importance than the technicalities of nomenclature after three hours of walking.

Chamorga really is the 'end of the line' as its bus terminus is also the end of the tarmac road, but at least it has a basic bar. Scanning the sharp ridges that surround the village and its steep *barranco* running down to the sea, you know that any circular walking route based on the village is going to be well up the 'exertion' rating. We offer this medium level great adventure taking us up to the saddle to stride along the **Anaga**'s airiest ridge to a spectacular viewing point, before descending on the traditional **Faro de Anaga** trail to the almost abandoned **Roque Bermejo** hamlet, with another option to descend to **Casas Blancas**. All those descents from the saddle have to be paid for on the final section as we ascend the spectacular *barranco* on an immaculate trail, the bar being a good incentive for tired legs during the long, seemingly endless, ascent! If you're fit enough for the terrain and only have time for one **Anaga** route then this should be your first choice.

| 4/5 | 4+ H | 9 km | ⛰ | ↗ 780m ↘ 780m | ↻ | 🍴 1 |

Access by car: From **El Bailadero** follow the twisty TF-123 and when it finally drops steeply off the ridge to park before the start of **Chamorga** village and walk in to our start point.

Access by bus: Bus N°247 bus leaves **Santa Cruz** at 05.00 (07.30 Saturdays) for the 60+ minute ride to **Chamorga**, returning from the village at 16.30 and 19.30; not really convenient times, so best by car.

From the parking area we stroll along **Chamorga**'s narrow street until it opens out at the bus terminus. A waypost (Wp.1 0M) directs us up a trail (N then NE) to curve above the bar and start a steady ascent up the northern wall of the *barranco* towards a 'dragon's head' rock. The views become even more impressive as we ascend and endemic flora crowds the steep slopes either side of our well-maintained trail as we reach the dragon's head (Wp.2 9M). Our trail turns into and contours round a floriferous side valley before climbing again. As our climb tops out at the head of the final stair (Wp.3 22M) it's back to easy walking as our narrow trail winds over the ridge (NE) to overlook the ruin of **Casa Tafada** on the saddle below us. A bit of a picky descent, not helped by abundant flora hiding small drops in the path, takes us to meet our Walk 45 (Wp.4) coming down the ridge line, shortly before we step onto the saddle (Wp.5 34M) and its path junctions.

Diversion

Most walkers, perhaps keen to get the kilometres in, take the broad, official *faro* trail along the northern side of the ruin but we'd encourage you to take a short diversion on **Montaña Tafada**. From the saddle (0M) we take a faint trail climbing along the ridge to a path junction (Wp.6) where we keep straight on. Views elsewhere on our route are impressive but from the

promontory at the end of the airy **Tafada** ridge (Wp.7 13M) they are nothing less than spectacular and include the vista down over our route; and look out for the dragon tree beside a rock arch.

Spectacular views from Wp.7

With a reasonable level of fitness you should complete the route even if you do arrive back at **Bar Chamorga** tired and the colour of boiled beetroot, but if you've any doubts about tackling 600 metres of descents and ascents now is the time to make your decision as we pick our way back along the rocky trail to the junction (Wp.6).

Continuation

Taking the path down off the ridge (0M) we have a steep, and very slippery when wet, descent through broom and tree heather to join the official *faro* trail (Wp.8 4M). Turning right (E), directions are superfluous as we follow the well-walked trail gently down across slopes simply packed with endemic flora. Dramatic islands come into view as we come down onto a rock sheet (Wp.9 12M) where small cairns guide us to our trail's continuation.

... alpine meadow slopes ...

We curve round below the bulk of **Tafada** and the *faro* comes into view, closer now but still a long way below us. After a natural rock seat (Wp.10 15M) our trail makes a serious rock descent with stepped and zigzag sections before running out across alpine meadow style slopes to take the line of a ridge running down from **Tafada**. In places the trail has a skittery surface making for slow progress relieved by views down into **Barranco Roque Bermejo** as we head for the lighthouse's cupola

And what views they are - just look at those cottages on top of a rock pillar way above the *barranco* floor, accessed by an intricate rock stair.

Our trail loses its skittery surface as we come to the 'Las Palmas' wayposted junction (Wp.11 53M) and on down to the fenced **Faro de Anaga** (Wp.12 56M), less impressive close to. From the *faro* a substantial dirt road winds down into the valley, a rather tiresome trudging descent zigzagging across

The dirt road down from the *faro*

The *ermita* at Roque Bermejo

steep barren slopes alleviated slightly by a short paved section before we reach the valley floor and a signed junction (Wp.13 73M). 'Las Palmas' is signed back the way we've come, 'Chamorga' is right while we follow the 'Roque Bermejo' sign down past cultivated plots to the almost abandoned hamlet and its *ermita* (Wp.14 77M).

Roque Bermejo might be Tenerife's most isolated community; we saw nobody but walkers and a hungry ginger cat. The *ermita* could do with some TLC but the messages inside to a recent walking accident death are a sage reminder not to be casual in our approach to these landscapes. You can continue down to **Casas Blancas**, either on the path across the valley floor or on the stepped descent from the *ermita*; after all you'll probably only be here once, so make the most of it. We missed out on **Casa Blancas** as we gave the concrete seats at the *ermita* a good sitting on while sharing our rations with the hungry cat, our excuse being that we were both recovering from heavy colds.

You can guess our final stage - yes, a slogging ascent up the *barranco* back to **Chamorga** (0M). It's quite a pull back up to the junction (Wp.13), then the steady ascent continues relentlessly. Remember that intricate stair we saw from the ridge line? It's instant recall as we start up its stepped ascent (Wp.15 13M), admiring views from the ruined cottages at the stair top (23M) after which we're back on more reasonable gradients. **Barranco de Roque Bermejo** is a beautiful ravine, the trail well maintained; in any other circumstances we'd extol its virtues as one of Tenerife's wonders. However today, probably because we're not 100% fit, we find it hard going and on rounding each twist and turn of the ravine we hope to see the white houses of **Chamorga** ahead, and each time we're disappointed. It's onwards and upwards, alleviated by a few gentler sections and frequent rests until finally a building comes into view (Wp.16 87M - our actual timing, slow for us proving they were pretty bad colds). Past the building - a hut - and up the trail to pass the first house (Wp.17 109M) with the heartening view of the village ahead.

After a 'Roque Bermejo' sign our trail widens into a dirt road which we follow up to the edge of the village (123M) where we intend to heartily support the rather impoverished local hostelry; as you step up from the tarmac the bar's toilets are on your left, allowing you wash off some of the grime and reduce the beetroot effect before tottering into **Bar Chamorga**.

GLOSSARY

a

abandonado	abandoned, in poor repair
abierto	open
acampamiento	camping
acantilado	cliff
agua	water
agua (no) potable	water (not) drinkable
alto	high
aparcamiento	parking
autopista	main road, motorway
ayuntamiento	town hall

b

bajo	low
barranco	ravine
bocadillo	bread roll
bodegón	inn
bosque	wood

c

cabezo	peak, summit
cabra	goat
caldera	collapsed cone (volcanic area)
calle	street
camino (particular)	trail, path, track (private)
camino real	old donkey trail (lit. royal road)
carretera	main road
casa	house
casa rural	country house accommodation to let
cascada	waterfall
caserío	hamlet, village
cementario	cemetery
cerrado	closed
cerveza	beer
choza	shelter
clinica	clinic, hospital
colmena	bee hive
comida	food
cordillera	mountain range
correos	post office
cortijo	farmstead
costa	coast
coto privado de caza	private hunting area
Cruz Roja	Red Cross (medical aid)
cuesta	slope
cueva	cave
cumbre	summit

d

degollado	pass
derecha	right (direction)
desprendimiento	landslide

e

embalse	reservoir
era	threshing circle
ermita	chapel
Espacio Naturaleza Protegido	protected area of natural beauty

estación de autobus/guagua — bus station

f

farmacia	chemist
faro	lighthouse
fiesta	holiday, celebration
finca	farm, country house
fuente	spring

g

gasolinera	petrol station
guagua	bus
Guardia Civil	police
guia	guide

h

hostal	hostel, accommodation
hoya	depression (geological)

i

iglesia	church
información	information
isla	island
izquierda	left (direction)

l

lago	lake
lavadero	laundry area (usually communal)
librería	bookshop
llano	plain
lluvioso	rainy
lomo	broad-backed ridge

m

malpais	'bad lands' wild, barren countryside
mapa	map
mercado	market
mirador	lookout/viewing point
montaña	mountain

n

nublado	cloudy

o

oficina de turismo	tourist office

p

parapente	hang-glider
peligroso	danger
pensión	guesthouse
pico	peak
picon	black volcanic rock/sand
pista	dirt road/track
pista (forestal)	forest road/track
playa	beach
plaza	square
policia	police
pozo	well
prohibido el paso	no entry
puente	bridge
puerto	port, mountain pass

r

refugio	refuge, shelter
río	river, stream
roque	rock
ruta	route

s		*tubería*	water pipe
salida	exit	**v**	
senda	path, track	*valle*	valley
sendero	foot path	*vega*	meadow
sierra	mountain range	*ventoso*	windy
sin salida	no through road/route	*volcán*	volcano
t		**z**	
tapas	bar snacks	*zona/área*	
teleférico	cable car	*recreativa*	recreation area
tienda	shop		
típico	traditional bar/eating place		
tormentoso	stormy		
torre	tower		
torrente	stream		

APPENDIX B: OTHER WALKING: SOME TRADITIONAL ROUTES

PICO DEL TEIDE - see Walk 40, page 160
Teleféricos (cablecars) are a wonderful way of climbing mountains, allowing even the least energetic to enjoy the same views as fit mountain walkers. You can walk up **Montaña Teide**, but it is one long hard slog with the rating for effort way off our scale. When you do get up there make sure you haven't forgotten your 'Pico' pass from Icona's office in Santa Cruz, or you won't be allowed up to the peak. (ICONA, Office Parque Nacional de Teide, Calle Emilio Calzadillo 5, 38002 Santa Cruz de Tenerife (00 34) 922 290129 & 922 290183; take a photocopy of your passport and request the date and time you wish to appear on the permit). If you must walk on **Mount Teide**, why not cablecar up and walk down, a long descent and tough on the knees. For a good description of both the ascent and descent of **Teide**, look at Mike Reid's website:-
www.fell-walker.co.uk/andalus.htm

MONTAÑA BLANCA
This is a popular ascent - only 400 metres compared to Teide's 1,400 metres. You can park by the start of the jeep track (limited parking) or a little further along the TF-21 by the k40 marker. Just keep slogging up the jeep track, following the crowds, and remember to go left onto **Montaña Blanca** when the masochists go right to continue their ascent on **Teide**. When you do get to the top, you'll have terrific views but it still feels a bit of a let down having the vast bulk of **Mount Teide** looming over you. Better by far in our opinion, is the ascent of **Montaña Guajara** (Walk 35) and the views from its plateau summit.

BARRANCO DEL INFIERNO
Once you could do this walk into the ravine of hell from upper **Adeje** anytime you wanted, but due to the popularity of this route and the resulting environmental wear and tear, the authorities now control numbers of visitors.

Phone (00 34) 922 782885 to ensure a booking, advisable for all and mandatory for groups of more than 12 together. There is a total limit of 200 visitors per day, with no more than 80 on the there-and-back trail at any one time. The walk is open from 8.30 a.m - 5.30 p.m daily and costs 3 euros per person. It's approximately 7km in total there and back and takes around 2½ hours, with climbs and ascents of 180 metres. Note that the waterfalls at the end of the walk are less than dramatic in summer and are best seen in late winter or early spring (December to March).